THE SUPERVISOR'S BOOKSHELF

General Editor: J. J. HENDERSON
Director, Institute of Supervisory Management

Industrial Relations

Industrial Relations

J. E. MORTIMER

*Editor of DATA Journal (Draughtsmen's
and Allied Technicians' Association)*

Published in association with the
INSTITUTE OF SUPERVISORY MANAGEMENT

HEINEMANN : LONDON

William Heinemann Ltd
LONDON MELBOURNE TORONTO
CAPE TOWN AUCKLAND

Printed in Great Britain
by Cox & Wyman Ltd,
London, Fakenham and Reading

Foreword

Greater recognition is being given to the job of the supervisor in industry, commerce, and the public service. His contribution to organizational efficiency and employee relations depends on how closely he is integrated into the management he serves. This, in turn, often depends on the skill and knowledge he displays in his work. Whilst company education and training schemes can help enormously in the development of talent, a lot depends on how much initiative the supervisor takes to equip himself for the tasks involved in his managerial role.

The purpose of this series of books on various aspects of management at the supervisory level is to give the go-ahead, alert minded supervisor a start in the right direction. No one can become a first-class supervisor by reading one or several books. The right personal qualities developed through a soundly based training scheme and directly linked to practical experience are essential. But this does not invalidate the point that a well-devised comprehensive series of educational books for supervisors can deepen and broaden their insight into supervisory management responsibilities and equip them to learn more quickly and thoroughly from experience.

The series, called *The Supervisor's Bookshelf*, provides (i) a comprehensive cover of essential subjects, (ii) supporting material for group discussions in I.S.M. local sections and company supervisors' associations, and (iii) additional texts for students reading for the examinations in Supervisory Studies. Each book has been specially commissioned and the individual authors are men with considerable experience of the work, the education and training, and the aspirations of supervisors.

Birmingham   J. J. HENDERSON

The Institute of
Supervisory Management

The Institute is a national body whose aim is to promote the appreciation of supervisory management as a profession through education, association, and research. It is concerned to establish and maintain the highest standards of qualification and performance. Membership services include local activities, publications, advice and information, appointments, courses, and conferences. The Institute of Supervisory Management is a self-supporting, voluntary association governed by a Council elected from its members. It is non-political and does not act as a negotiating body upon the question of salaries and wages.

Preface

The purpose of this book is to provide an outline of industrial relations. It was envisaged originally that it would serve mainly to assist persons who have a professional interest in the subject, namely supervisors and personnel officers. It was found, however, as the project proceeded that it might also be useful for students at universities, colleges of technology, and commercial and technical institutions who study industrial relations for educational purposes.

The plan of the book is fairly simple. It first introduces the reader to the social and legal framework of industrial relations. It is not, of course, a treatise on law. Nevertheless, anyone who is hoping to understand British industrial relations ought to try to grasp the main lines on which the law affecting trade unions and trade union activities has developed. This is particularly important for any discussion of current proposals for changes in the law affecting industrial relations. It is of special interest at the present time because of the enquiries of the Royal Commission on Trade Unions and Employers' Associations.

The book then proceeds to an outline of the structure of the British trade union movement and employers' organizations. Much has been written in the past about trade union structure but less about employers' organizations. Fortunately, the published evidence submitted to the Royal Commission has provided a new and reliable source of information.

The section of the book dealing with collective bargaining outlines not only the voluntary and statutory provisions but also discusses the incidence of strikes, the significance of unofficial and unconstitutional strikes, the development of workplace bargaining, the role of shop stewards, and the place of joint consultation.

The final section of the book discusses some current problems, including the effect of a national incomes policy on industrial relations, proposals which are being made for changes in the law affecting industrial relations, and the meaning and significance of restrictive practices.

I hope that this short book will prove useful not only to supervisors, personnel officers, and students but also to the general reader and not least to many members of trade unions.

J. E. MORTIMER

Contents

Contents

1: The Social and Legal Framework

The study of industrial relations is concerned with the practices and problems arising from the employment relationship between employer and worker. There are a number of distinguishing features of modern society which have made industrial relations a subject of special study. In the first place the majority of men and women in an industrial community – other than housewives who do not go out to work – are employed by others. They do not work in their own homes or on their own land; neither do they own the equipment or the materials with which they work. Most workers today are employed in a factory, workshop, transport undertaking, construction site or office owned by their employer. The employer also supplies most, and in many cases, all the equipment necessary for work. The contribution of the worker is to supply his labour. Labour, in this sense, is used in its widest meaning. It covers the effort of the labourer, the craftsmen, the technician, the scientist, and the manager; indeed, the effort of all who work for an employer.

The terms and conditions on which the worker is employed constitute his contract of employment. Every employed person, with the exceptions of those employed by the Crown, has such a contract. Civil Servants do not have a contract because the Crown is not subject to the normal law of the land and could not, therefore, be a party to a contract in the same way as other employers. Even this, however, is something of a fiction. For all practical purposes Civil Servants are employed under accepted conditions which have the effect of a contract of employment. Thus, for example, an established Civil Servant has no *right* to an occupational pension. The granting of the pension is subject to the discretion of the Crown. In fact, of course, an established Civil Servant can expect a pension with a degree of certainty no less than that of an employee in industry or commerce who is a member of an occupational scheme conducted by a reputable insurance company.

A contract of employment is nominally negotiated between two legally equal parties: the employer and the employee. In fact,

1

however, they are not equal. Their nominal equality in the eyes of the law is a myth. The employer is economically stronger than the individual employed person. He is usually wealthier, and when a worker goes to him for a job the employer can afford to haggle and to stand out for his price. The worker, on the other hand, is usually anxious to secure immediate employment. It is much less easy for him to insist on terms which the employer would not initially be prepared to accept.

Full employment or near full employment has undoubtedly strengthened the position of employees in their relationship with employers. If a worker possesses a skill which is scarce he may find that for a period at least he or she is able to move fairly freely between competing employers and to insist on better terms and conditions of employment. Even so, the standards by which the individual employee will judge his terms and conditions of employment will have been very largely determined for him according to the industry and locality in which he works. No individual employee – no matter how much his skill is in demand – is independent of the industrial and social environment in which he lives and works.

The Need to Combine

One of the main tasks of industrial relations is to study the means whereby terms and conditions of employment are determined. Nowadays in most industries this is done by collective bargaining. This term can best be understood by describing how collective bargaining developed.

From the earliest days of the industrial system workers felt the need to reduce the inequality of strength between themselves and their employer. They were brought to this view, in the first place, above all by the very bad terms and conditions under which they were employed. Their wages were low, their hours of labour were long, and they had no security against unemployment, industrial disease or injury.

The one obvious way in which they could strengthen their claim for improvements was to combine together. They could then ask collectively for better conditions. If their request were refused they could, as an ultimate measure, withdraw their labour and, by remaining together, eliminate the competition between themselves which hitherto has enabled their employer to exploit their labour.

2

Faced with a collective claim of this kind, backed, if necessary, by collective action, the employer might concede improved conditions. His main consideration would be the profitable continuity of his business. He might decide that it would be wiser to make a concession in order to bring about a return to normal working rather than to prolong a dispute for the sake of a relatively small sum. In any case, if he were a skilled manager he would be aware that high profits are much more likely to come from efficiency than from the crude exploitation of labour.

The need for workers to combine for the collective defence of their interests led to the formation of trade unions. Trade unions were formed to defend and advance the interests of working people. This remains their function to this day. Nowadays most claims and grievances in industry are settled by negotiation. This process of negotiation in which trade union representatives meet and bargain with employers is known as collective bargaining.

In the preceding paragraphs the process whereby trade unions came into existence has been described in very simplified terms. In fact the development of trade union consciousness among a substantial number of industrial workers was a long and in some respects a complicated process. It took years of experience before workers began to learn how to establish and maintain stable and permanent organizations. At first some of them were inclined to blind revolt and to destructive action. It was only later that their activity was directed mainly towards collective bargaining and the accumulation of funds for the payment of financial benefit to members who were unemployed, injured or in dispute with their employers.

The formation of employers' organizations came later than the development of trade unions. Employers' associations came into existence in many cases to combat trade unions and to provide for mutual assistance between employers when faced with a trade union claim for higher wages or a shorter working week. Early combinations of this kind were often short lived. They were formed to meet a specific claim or to deal with a particular problem. Once the immediate urgency had passed they went out of existence. It was only later – by which time many trade unions had already achieved a stable existence – that employers in a number of industries developed national organizations, not so much to oppose trade unionism as to participate in collective bargaining.

The Social Background

The British system of industrial relations is not something which is static. It is constantly developing. Nevertheless it now possesses certain characteristics which distinguish it from the systems of industrial relations in many other countries. One of its most essential characteristics is that employers and workers regulate their own relationship and that, in general, the State intervenes only to the extent necessary to encourage this self-regulation. This principle has been modified to a considerable extent in recent years with the introduction of new legislation on a range of matters affecting industrial relations, but it still remains true that on many issues employers and unions reach agreement without intervention by the State.

Another and related characteristic of the British system of industrial relations is that for the most part it is conducted outside the law. This does not mean that it is illegal. But it *does* mean that it is voluntary. There is no legal compulsion to organize, to negotiate, to reach agreement or even to observe agreements. (There are exceptions to these generalities and they will be described later but it is the essential characteristics with which this section is concerned.)

The main features of the British system of industrial relations are the outcome of history. It is only against the background of history that the significance of these features can be appreciated.

Towards the end of the eighteenth century, during the earliest years of the development of the industrial system, it was still the law in Britain that wages were fixed by the local Justices of the Peace. This provision had existed for hundreds of years and was contained in the Statute of Labourers of 1351 and the Statute of Apprentices of 1563. It followed that any combination of workers – and also any combination of employers – which sought to usurp this function of the magistrates was illegal. Nevertheless, the fixing of wage rates by local Justices of the Peace was quite unsuitable for industry. The local Justices could not be expected to understand the complexities of the new techniques; nor could they be expected to determine wage differentials for different grades of skill. Society was changing rapidly in the manufacturing towns, and the old methods of wage fixing could not be applied satisfactorily to the new industries.

The result was that in the manufacturing areas the local Justices more and more frequently neglected or deliberately declined to exercise their wage-fixing powers. Indeed, some of the earliest combinations of workmen had as their purpose the petitioning of local Justices to exercise their wage-fixing powers. Workers sometimes felt that if only the Justices would use their powers some measure of protection would be provided against exploitation by employers.

Sooner or later the law was bound to be brought into conformity with the needs of the Industrial Revolution. In 1813 and 1814 the laws relating to the fixing of wages by local Justices were repealed.

This, however, did not mean that trade unions were now legal. Towards the very end of the eighteenth century Parliament had passed the Combination Acts which provided a general prohibition on trade combinations. The motivation for this repressive legislation had been more political than industrial. The early trade societies were seen as the instrument through which the radical and democratic doctrines of the French Revolution might be imported, with subversive effect, into British society.

Trade combinations were also held to be in violation of the common law doctrine of freedom of trade. Under this doctrine – which formed part of the traditional unwritten law of the land – any association whose purpose was to impose restraints on trade was considered to be unlawful. Since one of the most important purposes of a trade union is to uphold wages and to prevent the employment of workers at wages below an agreed minimum it could be argued that trade unionism was in restraint of trade.

This doctrine of the illegality of trade restraints followed from the theory that the maximum social good would be achieved by permitting each citizen to pursue his own material interest without any kind of State intervention. According to this theory the mechanism of the market, namely the regulation of supply and demand by changes in price, would lead to the best possible distribution of resources between competing uses, provided that there was no artificial interference from outside. Thus, trade unionism, it was argued, would artificially interfere with the price of labour and in the long run would not assist the workers. It would be harmful to them because it would lead to less than the optimum distribution of economic resources. To put it in modern terms, trade unionism, whilst seemingly of advantage to the workers, would prove eventually to be disadvantageous because it would retard economic growth.

Despite these legal difficulties – represented by the common law, the traditional power of the Justices to fix wages, and the Combination Acts – the unions could not be totally suppressed. Time and again in the closing years of the eighteenth century and in the first two decades of the nineteenth century they appeared and reappeared on the social scene. Moreover, the extent to which the laws against them were vigorously applied varied very much from time to time and from place to place.

In the immediate period after the ending of the Napoleonic Wars the repression against any kind of movement for radical reform grew more severe. This was the period of the 'Peterloo Massacre' in 1819, when troops were used to break up a big demonstration of workers in Manchester. A number of demonstrators were killed.

The more far-sighted manufacturers and landed aristocracy recognized, however, particularly when trade improved, that a policy of severe repression might not be the wisest in the long term. It could possibly lead to revolution, whereas a policy of limited reform might quench the agitation for radical change, leaving the essential structure of the social system undisturbed.

In 1824 the Combination Acts were repealed. History books often refer to this repeal as the result of a parliamentary manœuvre. Undoubtedly the principal figure in the repeal, Francis Place, was a gifted tactician, but his efforts were successful because he was operating in circumstances more favourable to limited reform.

The Combination Laws Repeal Act, 1824, provided that combinations of workers or others for purposes of regulating wages and conditions should not be subject to proceedings for conspiracy. This Act led to such a growth in trade union organization that there were almost immediate demands for amending legislation. In the following year an amending Act was passed which curtailed the very limited rights given in the 1824 Act.

Nevertheless, the main breach in the wall of illegality had been made. Trade union organization extended among more and more workers. Even so, the unions had still to cope with formidable legal obstacles. In 1834 a group of Dorset agricultural labourers were sentenced to transportation to the penal colony of Australia for the crime of administering unlawful oaths at an initiation ceremony of the Friendly Society of Agricultural Labourers. They were eventually

6

brought back to England following a campaign of protest in which hundreds of thousands of people participated. They are commemorated today as the 'Tolpuddle Martyrs'.

After the passing of the Reform Act of 1832, which extended the vote to the better-off minority in the towns and ended some of the worst abuses of parliamentary representation, the main theme of working-class agitation was the demand for further parliamentary reform. The workers still had no share in democracy. The workers' demands were expressed in a six-point charter. The active members of the Chartist movement, as it was called, reasoned that if the workers could secure parliamentary representation through the extension of the franchise economic improvements would eventually follow.

With the rapid decline of Chartism after 1848 new forms of trade union organization assumed increasing importance. The new unions were based primarily upon skilled workers whose main concern was to share, with rising living standards, in the new prosperity made possible by the economic expansion of Victorian England. These new unions built up funds in years of prosperity to protect members against the hazards of unemployment and injury. Though most of these unions of skilled workers could trace their formation to the first half of the century they nevertheless had very little in common with the revolutionary spirit of Chartism. They represented such groups of workers as the skilled engineers, boilermakers, woodworkers, and moulders.

The Legislation of the 1870s

The law of the land was still very unsatisfactory for the proper functioning of the unions. They had secured the legal right to exist but their activities in relation, for example, to the fixing of minimum rates of pay were of doubtful legality. A major turning point came with new legislation in the 1870s. This legislation, strangely enough, was the outcome of an enquiry initiated with a view more towards restricting trade unionism than to granting it new legal rights. The enquiry took the form of a Royal Commission which was appointed following an outbreak of violence by a small group of trade union members in Sheffield.

The proceedings of the Royal Commission revealed that the main body of the trade union movement did not practise violence and,

7

indeed, that the new craft unions in particular were responsible bodies concerned exclusively with the regulation of employment conditions and the payment of benefits to protect members against unemployment and other hazards.

The Trade Union Act, 1871, is still of great importance for the study and practice of British industrial relations. Among its main provisions are the following:

Firstly, trade unions are not illegal because of their purpose in restraint of trade. Section 2 of the Act reads:

'The purposes of any trade union shall not, by reason merely that they are in restraint of trade, be deemed to be unlawful, so as to render any member of such trade union liable to criminal prosecution for conspiracy or otherwise.'

Secondly, trade union agreements in restraint of trade cannot be enforced at law. Similarly, the instructions of a union to its members, disciplinary measures, fines, and benefits are also not legally enforceable. Section 4 of the Act reads:

'Nothing in this Act shall enable any Court to entertain any legal proceeding instituted with the object of directly enforcing or recovering damages for the breach of any of the following agreements, namely,

(1) Any agreement between members of a trade union as such, concerning the conditions on which any members for the time being of such trade union shall or shall not sell their goods, transact business, employ or be employed;

(2) Any agreement for the payment by any person of any subscription or penalty to a trade union;

(3) Any agreement for the application of the funds of a trade union:

(*a*) To provide benefits to members; or

(*b*) To furnish contributions to any employer or workman not a member of such trade union, in consideration of such employer or workman acting in conformity with the rules or resolutions of such trade union; or

(*c*) To discharge any fine imposed upon any person by sentence of a court of justice; or

(4) Any agreement made between one trade union and another; or

8

(5) Any bond to secure the performance of any of the above-mentioned agreements.

But nothing in this section shall be deemed to constitute any of the above-mentioned agreements unlawful.'

Subsequent Court cases and legislation have, however, modified the apparent total exclusion of the Courts from any jurisdiction on these matters under the 1871 Act. When, for example, a trade union agreement forms part of the individual contract of employment of the worker the enforcement of the contract by or against the individual worker is *not* excluded from the jurisdiction of the Courts. No one can be really certain, however, whether this extends to the enforcement of negotiating procedure agreements. If the agreement is specifically referred to in the contract of employment it is probably enforceable. If it is not referred to, it might be held that it is no more than a voluntary arrangement which cannot be enforced by legal action. This, however, is an area of legal doubt.

It should be noted also that under the Terms and Conditions of Employment Act, 1959, provision is made by a special process for the enforcement upon a recalcitrant employer of recognized minimum terms and conditions of employment for a particular trade, industry or district.

Other legislation, including the Wages Councils Acts and the Agricultural Wages Act, also provide for the statutory enforcement of minimum wages and conditions for approximately four million workers. Legislation passed affecting other particular industries or sectors of employment also provides for the enforcement of minimum terms and conditions of employment.

The Courts have also been prepared – particularly in more recent years – to accept jurisdiction on complaints that the rules of a union have been broken or that 'natural justice' has not been observed when penalties have been imposed on members. The Courts have also accepted jurisdiction in cases concerning the deliberate falsification of union ballots. The Courts have not, however, assumed the power to decide whether or not a member should or should not be disciplined by his union for a breach of rules. They have confined themselves to the issue of whether or not the rules have been properly carried out, and whether or not the member accused of a breach of rules has been properly informed of the charge against him, has been given full opportunity to answer the charge, and whether the evidence so produced has been fairly considered by those who have imposed the penalty.

Thirdly, provision was made for the voluntary registration of trade unions with the Chief Registrar of Friendly Societies. Registered unions were given legal protection for their property and funds. This is probably the main advantage of registration.

Before 1871 Court decisions had given the unions little or no protection when officials, either full-time or lay, had defaulted with funds. Under the 1871 Act registration is open to any combination of persons provided that their main purpose is to regulate terms and conditions of employment and that they furnish to the Registrar a copy of their rules, which must include provision for electing the principal officers and executive body of the organization. The 1871 Act, it should be noted, does not give the Registrar legal authority to intervene on complaints that union rules are not being observed. Such authority is confined to the political rules of unions (*see* the Trade Union Act, 1913). In practice the Chief Registrar of Friendly Societies, though never exceeding his legal authority, is always most helpful to unions when advising them, in response to requests, about the operation of their rules.

In 1876 a Trade Union Act Amendment Act was passed to 'tidy up' the 1871 Act in the light of experience. It brought no fundamental changes except that it amended the definition of a trade union. The wording of the Trade Union Act, 1871, as amended by the Trade Union Act Amendment Act, 1876, does not confine the definition of a trade union to a combination of workmen. It can equally be a combination of employers, providing that its main purpose is to regulate terms and conditions of employment.

The definition reads:

'The term "trade union" means any combination, whether temporary or permanent, for regulating the relations between workmen and masters, or between workmen and workmen, or between masters and masters, or for imposing restrictive conditions on the conduct of any trade or business, whether such combination would or would not, if the principal Act had not been passed, have been deemed to have been an unlawful combination by reason of some one or more of its purposes being in restraint of trade.'

10

In 1913 this definition was further amended to provide that the above objects, together with the provisions of benefit to members, must be the principal objects of the organization.

Many employers' associations have availed themselves of the right to register as a trade union under the Trade Union Act, 1871. There are also a small number of trade unions – in the commonly accepted meaning of the term – which are not registered under the 1871 Act. One of them is the National Union of Teachers, which claims that its main purpose is the professional advancement of its members and that the regulation of the terms and conditions of employment of its members is subordinate to this main aim. The N.U.T. further claims that because it is not a trade union in the legal sense it is not subject to the Trade Union Act, 1913, which prescribes steps to be taken before a union can support candidates for public office. The N.U.T. has a sponsored list of parliamentary candidates but it has never observed the requirements of the 1913 Act.

Though the Trade Union Act, 1871, conferred new legal rights on trade unions another Act passed in the same year, the Criminal Law Amendment Act, 1871, codified and strengthened restrictions on trade union activities. Under this law heavy penalties could be imposed for intimidating or obstructing a person in order to coerce him for trade purposes. 'Obstruction' was so defined as to mean almost any attempt to persuade a worker to join a strike.

The trade unions campaigned strongly against this law and in 1875 another law was passed, the Conspiracy and Protection of Property Act, which – despite its title – considerably helped the unions. Its main provisions were:

Firstly, peaceful picketing was given legal protection. Section 6 of the Act made it clear that it was not unlawful to attend at a place of work 'in order merely to obtain or communicate information'.

Secondly, legal protection was given to any agreement or combination to take action in pursuit of a trade dispute unless such action if taken by an individual would have been punishable as a crime. The practical effect was to rule out the offence of 'conspiracy' for trade purposes.

Thirdly, it was made a criminal offence to break a contract of service, wilfully and maliciously, knowing that the probable consequence of so doing would be to endanger human life, cause serious bodily injury or expose valuable property to destruction, or serious

11

injury. Thus, for example, if a worker employed on a machine with-drew his labour without notice and knew, wilfully and maliciously, that the probable consequence of his action would be to endanger the life of, or cause serious bodily injury to, someone else, or to expose valuable property to destruction he could be charged with committing a criminal offence. The wording of the Act is, however, capable of wide interpretation. Such words as 'wilfully and maliciously','serious,' and 'valuable' are all somewhat indeterminate and leave plenty of room for legal argument.

This was and still is a particularly important legal provision affect-ing industrial relations. The effect of the 1875 Act was to make it clear that to break a contract of employment in a trade dispute, without wilfully and seriously endangering life or property, is *not* a crime. It may give rise to a civil action by an employer against work-men for breach of contract but it will not lead to a criminal prosecu-tion.

Even the possibility of civil action for breach of contract is, in the light of experience, unlikely. The damages awarded to an employer in such an action are likely to be small and, even more important, a great amount of ill will is likely to be created. Workers go on strike because they feel that they have a grievance, and if they are fined for their action their sense of grievance will probably increase rather than diminish. Moreover, the usual objective of an employer in an industrial dispute is to restore the normal profitable working of his enterprise. For an employer to take punitive legal action against men who will be working for him in the future is more likely to harm than to benefit his business.

Fourthly, it was made a criminal offence for a worker employed in gas or water supply to break a contract of service, wilfully and maliciously, knowing that his action would deprive consumers of their supply. In this respect employment in these public utilities was distinguished from other employment. This distinction was later extended to employment in electricity supply (Electricity Supply Act, 1919).

This provision does not mean that workers in public utilities are denied the right to strike. A strike by them is lawful providing they do not break their contracts of service, i.e. providing that they give proper notice of their intention to withdraw labour. Even, however, if they do not give proper notice it does not follow automatically that they have committed a criminal offence. It has still to be shown that they acted wilfully and maliciously knowing that their action would deprive consumers of their supply of gas, water or electricity.

The Trade Disputes Act, 1906

The next significant change in the legal framework affecting industrial relations was the Trade Disputes Act, 1906. This remains to this day the most important of all laws on trade union rights. It followed a legal decision of the House of Lords which made the funds of a trade union liable to claims for damages for actions taken on its authority. The Taff Vale Railway Company successfully took legal action against the Amalgamated Society of Railway Servants on the grounds that members of the union had conspired in a strike to induce workmen employed by the Company to break their contracts of employment and to interfere with traffic of the Company by unlawful means. The effect of this decision was to render practically worthless the nominal right to strike. As the unions were quick to point out, the purpose of a strike is to put pressure on an employer to induce or compel him to concede a claim which he could not be persuaded to concede by negotiations. The pressure is exerted by the workers withdrawing their labour. By this means they interfere with the trade of their employer. If a union is to be made liable to actions for damages for causing such interference the right to strike does not, in practice, exist.

The Taff Vale decision of the House of Lords in 1901 came as a surprise not only to the unions but also to many lawyers and to most people directly concerned with industrial relations. It was widely recognized that in some way or another the law would have to be changed if the right to strike were to be restored as a practical reality.

Following the Taff Vale judgment a vigorous campaign was conducted by the unions for a new law on trade disputes. With the election of a Liberal Government in 1906, and the appearance for the first time of a significant number of Labour Members in the House of Commons, new legislation was introduced to bring about the reform. The most important provisions of the Trade Disputes Act of 1906 were:

A trade union is not liable for wrongful acts committed by it or on its behalf. In other words, unions cannot be sued for civil wrongs. Section 4(1) of the Act reads:

'An action against a trade union, whether of workmen or masters, or against any members or officials thereof on behalf of themselves and all other members of the trade union in respect of any tortious act alleged to have been committed by or on behalf of the trade union, shall not be entertained by any Court.'

An act done in combination in pursuit of a trade dispute is not legally actionable if the act, without combination, would not be legally actionable. This had the effect of amending the law of conspiracy as it affected trade disputes. It gave protection to persons acting in combination in trade disputes against common law liabilities.

Peaceful picketing is legal. It is defined as follows in Section 2:

'It shall be lawful for one or more persons acting on their own behalf or on behalf of a trade union or of an individual employer or firm in contemplation or furtherance of a trade dispute, to attend at or near a house or place where a person resides or works or carries on business or happens to be, if they so attend merely for the purpose of peacefully obtaining or communicating information or of peacefully persuading any person to work or abstain from working.'

The clause on picketing in the Conspiracy and Protection of Property Act, 1875, was repealed.

It is lawful in pursuit of a trade dispute to induce a breach of an employment contract. Moreover, the fact that a particular act in pursuit of a trade dispute interferes with the trade, business or employment of some other person does not give grounds for legal action.

The Trade Union Act, 1913

The campaign to change the law following the Taff Vale judgment had brought the unions, to an unprecedented extent, into political activity. Many unions had used part of their funds to support the election to Parliament of candidates pledged to vote for new legislation. The unions assumed that this was a legitimate and legal extension of their normal activities.

In 1909 a railway worker, W. V. Osborne, a member of the Amalgamated Society of Railway Servants, took action against his society on the grounds that the use of trade union funds for political purposes was unlawful. The case was eventually taken to the House of Lords and a decision was given against the union.

The unions pressed strongly for new legislation to reverse this judgment. They argued that it was unfair because it placed working men at a disadvantage. Business interests, they said, were well represented in Parliament by Conservative and Liberal Members and the only practical way to secure independent labour representation was through trade union support.

Eventually, in 1913, a new Act was passed which went some way towards granting the unions what they wanted. The Trade Union Act, 1913, enables a union to include any lawful purpose in its constitution, including political objects, providing its principal objects are those of a trade union as defined in the 1876 Trade Union Act Amendment Act. If a union wishes to include political objects in its constitution it must satisfy a number of requirements. Firstly, it must take a ballot of its members and a majority must be obtained for political action. Secondly, it must set up a separate political fund from which all expenditure for prescribed political objects must be made. Thirdly, it must provide for any member who does not wish to contribute to the political fund to 'contract out'. Fourthly, any member who exercises his legal right to 'contract out' must not be placed in any less favourable position in relation to any rights of membership except in relation to the control of the political fund.

The statutory political objects set out in the Trade Union Act, 1913, are as follows:

'The political objects to which this section applies are the expenditure of money:

(a) On the payment of any expenses incurred either directly or indirectly by a candidate or prospective candidate for election to Parliament or to any public office, before, during, or after the election in connexion with his candidature or election; or

(b) On the holding of any meeting or the distribution of any literature or documents in support of any such candidate or prospective candidate; or

(c) On the maintenance of any person who is a member of Parliament or who holds a public office; or

(d) In connexion with the registration of electors or the selection of a candidate for Parliament or any public office; or

15

(e) On the holding of political meetings of any kind, or on the distribution of political literature or political documents of any kind, unless the main purpose of the meetings or of the distribution of the literature or documents is the furtherance of statutory objects within the meaning of this Act.

'The expression "public office" in this section means the office of member of any county, county borough, district, or parish council or board of guardians, or of any public body who have power to raise money, either directly or indirectly, by means of a rate.'

It should be noted that the statutory political objects do not preclude trade unions from spending their normal funds on issues which may have a strong political connotation but concern the regulation of relations between employers and workers. Thus, for example, unions do not regard themselves as prohibited from spending their normal funds in holding meetings or making representations to Ministers about, say, legislation on factory safety or on prices and incomes. Money used, however, to support sponsored parliamentary candidates is always taken from the political fund. (The exception is the National Union of Teachers – see earlier paragraphs – which claims not to be a trade union.)

Legislation in the 1920s

In the years immediately following the First World War there were a number of large-scale industrial disputes. During one of these disputes in the mining industry, when sympathetic action by other workers appeared likely, Parliament passed the Emergency Powers Act, 1920. It has been used on a number of occasions in industrial disputes. It empowers the Government to declare a state of emergency if it appears that action is being taken or is threatened which is likely to deprive the community or any substantial part of it with the essentials of life, notably food, water, fuel, light or the means of transport. When a state of emergency has been declared under this Act the Government can make regulations for securing the essentials of life to the community.

There are a number of safeguards written into the Emergency Powers Act to prevent its being used for other than securing the essentials of life to the community. The Government cannot make

16

regulations under the Act to introduce compulsory military service, industrial conscription, or to make strike action illegal.

In 1927, following the General Strike of the previous year, legislation was introduced which curtailed trade union rights. It was, however, completely repealed in Great Britain in 1946. Nevertheless, it still exists in Northern Ireland. The main provisions of the Trade Disputes and Trade Unions Act, 1927, were:

A strike or lockout was illegal if its purpose was other than or in addition to the furtherance of a trade dispute, and if it was intended to coerce the Government either directly or by inflicting hardship upon the community.

Protection was given only to trade disputes between employers and workmen in a specific trade or industry. Sympathetic strikes by workers in another trade or industry were thus no longer given legal protection.

The definition of peaceful picketing was changed. In practice this meant that almost any attempt to picket workers to join a strike might run foul of the law.

The procedure of 'contracting in' was substituted for 'contracting out' for contributions to union political funds under the Trade Union Act, 1913.

Established Civil Servants were precluded from becoming members of unions which included workers outside the Civil Service, or which had political objects, or which were affiliated to any other industrial or political organization. A number of Civil Service unions had to leave the T.U.C.

Non-unionists employed by public authorities were not to be placed at any disadvantage either directly or indirectly.

Public authorities were not permitted to make it a condition of any contract that there should be 100 per cent trade union membership.

Recent Legislation
In 1963 the House of Lords made a decision in the Rookes versus Barnard case, concerning draughtsmen at London Airport, which modified what had hitherto been generally regarded as the interpretation of the 1906 Trade Disputes Act. Previously it had been the

general view that a threat to take strike action in breach of a contract of employment but in pursuit of a trade dispute was protected.

The House of Lords decided that the 1906 Act did not protect a threat to take strike action in breach of a contract of employment and damages were awarded to Mr Rookes who had been dismissed from his employment following such a threat. The union involved alleged that Mr Rookes had resigned from the union when he had been unable to persuade his office colleagues to agree with him as to the manner in which a grievance should be pursued. The union, with the support of the majority of its members – there was 100 per cent membership – wanted to pursue the grievance through the constitutional machinery. When Mr Rookes resigned from the union the other draughtsmen, with the support of their union, threatened to strike unless the employing authority, BOAC, withdrew Mr Rookes from the office. In response to this threat BOAC at first suspended Mr Rookes and later dismissed him. It was an important feature of the case that, though 100 per cent trade union membership in the office where Mr Rookes worked was 'recognized' by the management, there was also a 'no strike' clause in the procedure agreement between the employing authorities in civil air transport and the unions. The terms of this agreement had been supplied to each worker and it was held that they constituted part of the contract of employment.

The Rookes versus Barnard decision resulted in considerable controversy. The unions took the view that if a threat to take strike action was now legally actionable the right to strike had been seriously prejudiced. The practical effect, they argued, would be to encourage lightning strikes for there would then be no threat of strike action. Supporters of the House of Lords judgment argued, on the other hand, that the Law Lords' decision was a necessary corrective to the intimidation of non-unionists by trade unionists.

In 1965 Parliament passed a new Trade Disputes Act which restored to the unions the protection which they previously thought they possessed under the Trade Disputes Act, 1906. It gives protection to persons who in the course of a trade dispute threaten or induce others to threaten to break a contract of employment.

Although the traditional role of the law in industrial relations in Britain has been to provide no more than a framework in which employers and trade unions could lawfully carry out their respective functions, there has been a significant development in recent years in the introduction of new legislation to promote better standards of employment for all workers and not only for those in 'sweated' trades. This new legislation has extended beyond the protection of the safety and health of the worker for which, there is a long tradition.

In 1963 the Contracts of Employment Act was passed by Parliament. It gives both employers and employees rights to minimum periods of notice to terminate employment and it places a duty on employers to give their employees written particulars of their main terms of employment. An employer is required to give an employee a minimum of 1 week's notice if the employee has been with him continuously for 26 weeks or more; a minimum of 2 weeks' notice if the employee has been with him continuously for 2 years or more; and a minimum of 4 weeks' notice if the employee has been with him continuously for 5 years or more. An employee is required to give his employer a minimum of 1 week's notice if he has worked for him continuously for 26 weeks or more. The minimum period of notice does not increase with longer service.

The minimum periods of notice under the Contracts of Employment Act do not apply to part-time employees who work less than 21 hours a week; nor do they apply to dockers, merchant seamen, Crown servants, and certain employees with fixed-term contracts. The right to minimum periods of notice under the Act applies in all normal circumstances, but a contract of employment can be terminated without notice if the behaviour of the other party justifies it. Under an amendment to the Act introduced in 1965, strikes in breach of contract are no longer regarded as breaking the period of continuous employment for the purpose of calculating the entitlement to minimum notice.

The Act requires that employers must give to their employees written information about their main terms of employment. This includes the rate of pay, piecework and overtime rates, hours of work, holidays and holiday pay, sickness and sick pay, pensions and pension schemes, and periods of notice to terminate employment. This written information has to be given to an employee not later than 13 weeks after his employment has begun. Any subsequent changes have to be notified to the employee or the information must be available to him in readily available reference documents (e.g. collective agreements).

In 1964 the Industrial Training Act was passed by Parliament. Its purpose is to help in producing an adequate supply of properly trained men and women at all levels in industry, to improve industrial training, and to provide for sharing the cost of training more evenly between firms. The Minister of Labour is empowered to establish industrial training boards with a chairman and representative members, appointed by the Minister, from employers, trade unions, and the field of education. A number of such boards have already been established.

Each board is responsible for making proposals for training in the industry which it covers. In addition it submits proposals for Ministerial approval for the raising of a training levy on the firms in the industry. Firms whose training courses are approved receive a grant from the board. The scheme for levies and grants thus encourages firms to provide proper training.

In the following year, in 1965, Parliament passed another measure to improve minimum standards for all employees. This time it was the Redundancy Payments Act. This Act stipulates that employers must make lump-sum payments to employees who are dismissed because of redundancy. The amount of the payment is calculated by reference to the employee's pay, length of service with the employer, and age.

For the purpose of the Act a dismissed employee is regarded as redundant when the whole or main reason for his dismissal is that his employer's needs for employees to do work of a particular kind have diminished or ceased. The Ministry of Labour's official booklet on the redundancy payments scheme explains that it makes no difference why the employer needs fewer employees – this may be, for example, because he is closing down, either altogether or in a particular area, or because of a trade recession, or because of a change in production arrangements. In all these cases, if the result is that the employer needs fewer employees then those employees who have been dismissed have been dismissed because of redundancy.

To qualify for a redundancy payment from an employer, an employee must have served continuously with him for 2 years. Service before the employee's eighteenth birthday does not count. A redundant employee with at least 2 years' service is entitled to a $\frac{1}{2}$ week's pay for each year of service between ages 18 and 21 inclusive; 1 week's pay for each year of service between ages 22 and 40 inclusive; and $1\frac{1}{2}$ weeks' pay for each year of service between ages 41 and 64 (59 for women) inclusive. Male employees aged 65 and female employees aged 60 are not entitled to a redundancy payment. For employees who are nearing these ages when they become redundant there is a progressive reduction in redundancy payments. When an employer provides a pension or lump-sum superannuation payment to a redundant employee under the age of 65 (60 for women) he may, if he so chooses, reduce or eliminate the redundancy payment on a scale determined by the Ministry.

When calculating redundancy pay, earnings over £40 per week are disregarded. Redundancy payments are related to the number of complete years of continuous employment, up to a maximum of twenty years, reckoning backwards from the date on which the employee's contract is terminated. The maximum redundancy payment is £1,200. This would be received by a man with a weekly pay of £40 who had served twenty continuous years with an employer from the age of 41 years.

The Redundancy Payments Act also establishes a Redundancy Fund, financed by contributions. When employers make payments to redundant employees they can claim rebates from the Fund, ranging from two-thirds to just over three-quarters of the amount they pay out.

Discussion has also taken place in recent years on other legislative proposals on conditions of employment. There have, for example, been suggestions for legislation on equal pay for equal work between men and women and legislation to provide redress against unjustified of arbitrary dismissal.

In 1965 the Government appointed a Royal Commission on Trade Unions and Employers' Associations. The decision to appoint a Royal Commission followed wide public discussion of the relationship of the law to trade union activities and the role of unions and employers' organizations in modern society. The terms of reference of the Royal Commission were as follows:

'To consider relations between managements and employees and the role of trade unions and employers' associations in promoting the interests of their members and in accelerating the social and economic advance of the nation, with particular reference to the law affecting the activities of these bodies; and to report.'

When this chapter was written the Royal Commission had not yet reported, though it had taken a great amount of evidence.

2: The Structure of Trade Unions and Employers' Associations

There are about 10 million trade union members in Britain. The total number of employees is over 23 millions so that less than one-half are trade union members. It has been estimated that somewhere between 55 per cent and 60 per cent of male employees but only about 25 per cent of female employees are trade union members. The proportion of young workers under 21 who are trade union members is also below the national average for all workers.

The number of trade unions has declined fairly sharply over the years, but there are still nearly 600 in existence. There is an enormous variation in size. More than half the unions in Britain have less than 1,000 members each. They represent no more than 1 per cent of the total number of trade union members. At the other extreme the three largest unions, the Transport and General Workers' Union, the Amalgamated Union of Engineering and Foundry Workers, and the National Union of General and Municipal Workers, represent between them about one-third of all trade union members in Britain. The Transport and General Workers' Union alone has a membership of more than 1,450,000.

The concentration of membership in the large unions is further illustrated by the fact that the eight largest unions organize between them more than one-half of all trade union members in Britain. The largest thirty-five unions organize between them more than 80 per cent of all trade union members.

There are also very wide variations in the degree of trade union organization between different industries, services, and occupations. On the one hand there are industries where virtually every manual worker is a trade union member. They include coal-mining, shipbuilding, and port transport. There is also a fairly high level of trade union organization among non-manual workers in the coal-mining industry and among technical staff in shipbuilding. Other industries or services in which there is a much higher than average level of

22

trade union organization are iron and steel, cotton and footwear manufacture, printing, railways, docks, public road transport, the Civil Service, and local government.

On the other hand there are a number of industries and services in which only a relatively small minority of the workers are organized. They include agriculture, distribution, insurance, food and drink manufacture and processing, sections of the chemical industry, and sections of the textile industry other than cotton manufacture.

Significant industries which lie somewhere between the two extremes are engineering and electrical goods manufacture, building and construction, gas, electricity, and water services, and education.

In the period since the ending of the Second World War there has also been a marked change in the distribution of trade union membership between different industries. This has corresponded to the decline of coal-mining, railways, and cotton textiles, and to the expansion of the engineering and subsidiary industries, transport other than railways, and the public services. There has also been a marked growth of trade union organization among white-collar employees. Another significant trend has been the expansion of the Transport and General Workers' Union, whose membership extends over a wide range of industries and occupations.

Even in industries which are well organized it is not unusual to find that a particular section or occupational group is poorly organized. This is often the case, for example, with clerical employees in private industry. It has also been found difficult to maintain a high and stable level of trade union organization among labourers in the building and construction industries. The movement of labour from site to site and the tendency for building labourers to move into other occupations makes it much more difficult for the unions to achieve effective and permanent organization. The growth of 'self-employment' in the building industry, even among workpeople who by normal standards would be regarded as employed persons, has also undermined the traditional strength of trade union organization among building craftsmen. In some industries it is also not unusual to find differences in the level of trade union organization even among skilled workers. In engineering, for example, the degree of organization among sheet metal workers is very high. In hotels, although the great majority of workers are unorganized, it is not unusual to find that the maintenance craftsmen, including electricians, carpenters, and heating engineers, are members of their appropriate unions.

It is customary to divide British trade unions into four categories: craft unions, industrial unions, general workers' unions, and white-collar unions. This division, however, has to be treated with a great deal of caution. British trade unions do not conform to any rigid organizational principles. Unions have grown, developed, and some-times merged with each other according to the pressure of historical circumstance and the day-to-day needs and wishes of their members. The result is a bewildering variety of forms of organization. Never-theless, a description based upon a division of British unions into craft, industrial, general workers', and white-collar organizations helps to distinguish some of the main trends of development.

Craft Unionism

Craft unions, consisting of skilled workmen following the same trade and recruited on a local basis, were among the first trade unions to be formed in Britain. Many of them had only a temporary existence. They were formed often to deal with an immediate grievance and when the grievance was resolved they went out of existence. Some of them also suffered from legal repression or the hostility of employers. They were destroyed or driven underground. Nevertheless, a few of these organizations took permanent root in the first half of the nineteenth century. Among them, for example, were the local organizations which later came together to form the Amalgamated Society of Engineers and the Boilermakers' Society.

Some of the craft unions in engineering, shipbuilding, building, printing, and cotton textiles greatly strengthened their position in the second half of the nineteenth century. These unions had two main functions. The first was to bargain collectively with employers on behalf of their members. They were able to obtain some share for their members from the rewards of industrial expansion in Victorian Britain. For the most part the craft unions of the time were strongly committed to a policy of industrial peace. They regarded it as the hallmark of good leadership to avoid, almost at any cost, spending money on industrial disputes.

Their second main function was to provide financial protection for their members against the hazards of unemployment and indus-trial accident, and to provide a limited superannuation payment to members in retirement. In the years before the introduction of State unemployment benefit and State old-age pensions the donations made by craft unions were the principal form of benefit received by their unemployed and retired members. The importance of these financial benefits encouraged the craft unions to conserve their funds and to pursue a policy of conciliation with the employers.

Because of the need to exercise strict control over their funds the craft unions in the second half of the nineteenth century developed centralized systems of management and administration. Some of the early leaders of the craft unions were extremely able and dedicated men, and contributed enormously to the development of a tradition of stability, 'respectability', and craft solidarity. These traditions remain to this day important for an understanding of the British trade union movement.

Despite its important contribution to the development of the trade union movement in Britain, craft unionism suffers from a number of weaknesses. In the first place craft divisions do not remain the same. Changes take place in industry and new techniques are developed. Crafts, which at one time appeared to be unchanging, are undermined by new tools, machinery, and methods. Above all the clear distinction which existed between skilled craftsmen and labourers in the middle years of the last century has become more and more blurred. In industries where mass production methods are now employed the majority of workers are neither skilled craftsmen in the nineteenth-century sense nor labourers. They are semi-skilled operatives, whose skill extends over only a narrow range of functions.

This does not, of course, imply that all crafts are steadily being destroyed by industrial development. The introduction of new methods and techniques has not only undermined certain of the old crafts; it has also brought a demand for craftsmen of a new type. Thus the introduction of batch production and mass production methods has greatly increased the demand for toolmakers. It has also increased very substantially the demand for technicians of various kinds. These technicians usually have a high level of skill and are concerned more with designing, planning, estimating, calculating, and work study than with manual operations.

In some industries the most highly productive firms and those which employ the most modern techniques require only a small proportion of skilled craftsmen among their total labour force. These same firms, however, because they are highly productive are also able to pay the highest wages in the industry. Hence some semi-skilled workers employed in these highly productive firms are able to obtain wages considerably higher than the wages paid to craftsmen in other but less productive sections of the same industry. This is a familiar problem in engineering. The average level of earnings in motor-car production, for example, is substantially higher than in some other sections of the engineering industry where a higher proportion of skilled workers are employed.

The other major weakness of craft unionism is that no one group of craftsmen, no matter how strongly organized they may be, can, in the long run, be indifferent to the welfare of other workpeople employed in the same industry. Indeed, in modern large-scale industry employers understandably favour standard conditions for all employees on such matters as hours of work, holidays, sickness pay entitlement, and provisions for retirement. If a craft union represents only a minority of workers in an industry and the majority remain unorganized the standard conditions likely to be established will be influenced by the absence of trade union organization among most of the workers.

In modern industry too the interdependence of processes tends to promote among workers a sense of industrial identity. By the very nature of their day-to-day occupation workpeople in different groups come to recognize that their interests are bound up with the interests of other workpeople in the same industry.

It is not surprising, therefore, that over the years craft unionism, though it still plays an important part in British trade unionism, has not proved satisfactory as the basis for the organization of the *majority* of British workers. Most craft unions which developed in the nineteenth century have found it necessary to introduce important changes in their forms of organization. Many early craft unions have amalgamated with unions catering for related trades. This process is still continuing. Within recent years, for example, the unions of boilermakers, blacksmiths, and shipwrights, have amalgamated to form one union whilst preserving a measure of trade autonomy for each craft. Similarly, in the founding industry, the main union, known till recently as the Amalgamated Union of Foundry Workers, took shape as a result of a succession of amalgamations. More recently the A.U.F.W. decided to amalgamate with the Amalgamated Engineering Union and to become a trade section of a broader engineering union, now known as the Amalgamated Union of Engineering and Foundry Workers. In printing, the unions of skilled men, organized both for different crafts and for different areas, eventually came together to form one national union, the National Graphical Association. In building, some of the craft unions among bricklayers and masons amalgamated to form the Amalgamated Union of Building Trade Workers and again, more recently, further discussions have been taking place to form one union for all trowel trades.

There are still many important unions in Britain which are organized on a craft basis or whose membership is restricted almost entirely to skilled men. Some of the unions mentioned in the last paragraph, though they now embrace a number of crafts, are still confined to skilled workers. In addition, there are unions like the United Patternmakers' Association, the Sheet Metal Workers' Society, and the Operative Spinners in cotton textiles which still play a very important part in their respective industries. On the railways, the majority of engine drivers and firemen are members not of the National Union of Railwaymen but of the Associated Society of Locomotive Engineers and Firemen, which organizes on a strictly occupational basis. Among white-collar employees a number of unions catering for skilled technicians have also grown rapidly in recent years. Among such unions, the Draughtsmen's and Allied Technicians' Association and the Electrical Power Engineers' Association are both well-organized and effective bodies.

Some of the unions which in the last century organized strictly on a craft basis have widened their field of recruitment to include semi-skilled and even unskilled workers in the same industry. This evolution has nearly always been accompanied by a sharp controversy within the union. Those who resisted the change argued that the recruitment of semi-skilled and unskilled workers would dilute the membership and lower the esteem in which the union was held, both by its existing members and by employers. They also argued that the recruitment of less skilled workers might threaten the financial stability of the union in a period of industrial depression. Those who argued for the widening of the scope of recruitment were able to point to the growing number of semi-skilled workers employed in the firms where the craft union had its membership. They were able to

27

show that highly skilled craftsmen were becoming a smaller proportion of the total labour force, and that nowhere was this so apparent as in the expanding firms employing the most modern techniques of production. If the semi-skilled workers were to be left unorganized the conditions of the craftsmen would ultimately be threatened.

Perhaps the best example of this change from a narrow craft basis of organization to a wider industrial basis is provided by the Amalgamated Union of Engineering and Foundry Workers. In the last century the main unions in engineering, which later formed the A.U.E.F.W. organized on a strictly craft basis. Stage by stage, however, decisions were taken, following keen debate, in favour of the recruitment of semi-skilled and finally unskilled workers and women.

To this day, nevertheless, the A.U.E.F.W. is strongly influenced by its craft traditions. The skilled men tend to be by far the most influential in the union, and in some areas the local representatives of the union are less than enthusiastic about recruiting all workers who are eligible under the rules. In some sections of the engineering industry, particularly those which have developed rapidly during this century, the A.U.E.F.W. represents only a proportion of those who today would be eligible for membership under its existing rules. Tens of thousands of workers in these modern industries are members of other unions, particularly the Transport and General Workers' Union.

Industrial Unionism

An industrial union is one which seeks to organize all workers within a given industry, irrespective of their skill, occupation or sex. It confines its organization to the one industry and does not seek to extend its membership elsewhere.

There are no perfect examples of industrial unionism in the British trade union movement. There are, however, a number of unions which are organized mainly on industrial lines and have been and remain strongly influenced by the strength of the arguments for for industrial unionism. They include, to name only a few, the National Union of Mineworkers, the National Union of Railwaymen, the National Union of Boot and Shoe Operatives, the National Union of Agricultural Workers, and the National Union of Seamen.

The case for industrial unionism rests on the desirability, from a trade union point of view, of uniting in one union all workpeople employed within a single industry. Those who favour industrial unionism claim that if all workers in one industry are in the same union it is not then possible for employers to play off one group against another. Nor is it possible for one group of workers in a particularly favourable position to exploit their advantage to the detriment or neglect of the interests of other groups of workers in the same industry. Those who favour industrial unionism also point out that if all workers in an industry, irrespective of craft, are in one union there is less likelihood of demarcation disputes about who should do this or that job.

Some industrial unionists also stress that one of the principal advantages of industrial unionism is that it promotes the solidarity of all workers. This, they say, is desirable not only for trade union effectiveness in collective bargaining but also for the broader social purposes of trade unionism. Industrial unionism, it is argued, encourages workpeople to have regard not only to their own immediate interest but also to the wider interest of the industry in which they are employed and to the welfare of all workpeople whose livelihood depends on the industry.

One of the problems of industrial unionism is that it is impossible in most industries to define exactly where one industry begins and another ends. If, for example, a road transport undertaking or a cross-Channel shipping line is owned by British Rail does it form part of the railway industry? Or should the workers in the road transport undertaking be members of a road transport workers' union and the workers in the cross-Channel shipping line be members of a seamen's union? Or to take another example: if a motor-car firm has its own metal producing plant should the workers employed in it be members of the main union organized in the motor-car industry or should they be members of, say, the main union for the iron and steel industry? Or yet another example: is a printing plant, owned by a large chemical combine and employed exclusively in printing advertising material and packages for chemicals, part of the printing industry or of the chemical industry? There is and can be no clear-cut answer to these and many similar problems.

Even within industries where there are strong industrial unions, as, for example, coal-mining and railways, there are still groups of workpeople who have insisted on remaining members of their own craft or occupational unions. Mention has already been made of the existence of ASLEF in railway employment. In the railway workshops many workers are members of the N.U.R.

Some skilled workers also feel that industrial unionism does not provide adequate protection for their distinguishable trade interests. This does not necessarily mean that they are indifferent to the welfare of other workers in the same industry. They insist, however, that they have certain separate problems and interests which are not necessarily in conflict with, but are distinguishable from, the interests of other workers in the industry. They often argue that a craft union is able to provide them with better service than an industrial union.

Though industrial unionism cannot provide an answer to all of the needs of trade unionists and the problems of the trade union movement – as is shown by the strength of unions in Britain based on other than industrial principles of organization – it does satisfy one basic need of trade unionism. It provides for the representation of the collective interests of workers employed within the same industry. It may be difficult or even impossible to define exactly what constitutes an industry but, nevertheless, there are clearly many firms which can be grouped together and whose workpeople have a common interest. The concept of industrial unionism, despite the difficulties of defining an industry, is not meaningless. Hence even in those industries where an industrial union has not evolved, some other form of organization has had to be created to provide for the common industrial interests of workers. This has usually taken the form of a federation of trade unions (this is described more fully below).

General Unionism

A special feature of the British trade union movement is the strength of the general workers' unions. There are two main general workers' unions in existence and a third which has some of the features of a general union. The first two are the Transport and General Workers' Union, which is the largest union in Britain, and the National Union of General and Municipal Workers, which is the third largest. The union with some of the features of a general union is the Union of Shop, Distributive, and Allied Workers. It is the sixth largest union in Britain. The fact that three of the six largest unions in Britain are general workers' organizations is an indication of the success of this type of trade union organization in meeting the needs of a considerable section of the British labour force.

There are a number of reasons for the extensive membership and growth of the general workers' unions. Each of them is well organized in one or more industries. This serves as their base and has given them stability. It helps them to extend their organization into other fields. The basic strength of the Transport and General Workers' Union is in docks and in road transport; that of the National Union of General and Municipal Workers is in the public utilities and in shipbuilding, chemicals, and glass manufacture; and that of the Union of Shop, Distributive, and Allied Workers is among Co-operative employees.

There are many industries in Britain which are too small to sustain an industrial union. Some of these industries employ only a small proportion of skilled men: the majority of the workers are either semi-skilled or unskilled operatives. Many of the workers in these industries are also women. The general workers' unions were able to extend trade union organization into many of these industries. But for the general unions the workers in these industries would not have been organized; probably no other form of organization would have been successful.

The case for the general workers' unions was put by the T.G.W.U. and N.U.G.M.W. in their evidence to the Royal Commission on Trade Unions and Employers' Associations. The T.G.W.U. said:

'They must be large enough to bargain effectively for their members over the whole area in which they are employed, and they must be able to give the kind of service – including specialized technical, legal, research, and educational provision – that is necessary if members' interests are to be promoted effectively.'

The N.U.G.M.W. said:

'Horizontal organization in many ways conforms more to the realities of the structure of British industry, and with the increased likelihood of the further growth in the size and number of large multi-industry firms it is also likely that horizontal organization will increasingly fit industrial circumstance better than exclusively industrial organization. We consider that general unionism can provide a framework within which a variety of circumstances can be accommodated and the industrial and occupational interests of workers can be efficiently safeguarded and promoted.'

31

The Union of Shop, Distributive, and Allied Workers found from its practical day-to-day experience that it was necessary to extend trade union organization into areas which it probably did not at first seek to cover but which were related to distribution. Nowadays USDAW organizes not only among wholesale and retail distributive workers, including administrative and clerical staff, but also 'such productive and manipulative workers who are employed in separate establishments or in premises ancillary to distributive departments as may be determined from time to time'.

This 'open-ended' approach to trade union recruitment is a feature of most of the unions which have shown a significant rate of growth in recent years. One commentator, Mr John Hughes, Lecturer in Economics and Industrial Relations at Ruskin College, Oxford, has said, 'It does not look, therefore, as if trade unions with rapidly growing membership demonstrate any natural evolution to industrial unionism. Rather it is an extension of (overlapping) general unionism, and occupational unionism that is mainly in evidence.'

There are important differences in structure between the T.G.W.U. and the N.U.G.M.W. The Transport and General Workers' Union has a trade group structure. There are trade groups covering, among others, docks, road transport passenger services, road transport commercial services, engineering and shipbuilding, construction, Government workers, municipal workers, chemicals, administrative, clerical, and supervisory workers, and general workers. The trade groups are directly represented on the General Executive Council of the Union. The General Executive Council also includes regional representatives who are elected by ballot vote of the membership within each region, irrespective of trade. There are thirteen territorial regions in the Union. The policy of the Union on broad general issues is determined by a biennial delegate conference which consists of about 800 delegates elected by and from regional trade groups on a membership basis. The biennial delegate conference does not deal with specific trade matters, but concerns itself with the report of the General Executive Council and motions concerning broad general policy and the administration of the Union. Trade matters are normally dealt with by national trade group committees.

The National Union of General and Municipal Workers, on the other hand, puts more emphasis in its structure on district control. There are no national trade groups within the Union. Each branch in the Union – and there are more than 2,200 of them – comes under the jurisdiction of a district. There are ten districts within the structure of the Union. Each district has a District Council elected every two years from the branches. The District Council meets twice a year and elects a District Committee. The District Committee has considerable authority under the rules of the Union and is obliged to meet every four weeks but can meet more frequently if it so wishes. The District Councils and Committees are responsible for the making of policy on matters affecting their own district. Supreme authority in the Union is vested in an annual delegate congress whose delegates are elected on a branch and district basis. Beneath the annual delegate congress is a General Council consisting of the Chairman of the Union, the General Secretary, the ten district secretaries, and fourteen lay members elected by the districts. The General Council meets at least once every three months. The General Council appoints a National Executive Committee, consisting of one representative from each district, half of whom must be lay members. The National Executive Committee meets at least once a month.

The general workers' unions are represented on a large number of national negotiating bodies. The N.U.G.M.W. is represented on at least 145 and the T.G.W.U. on even more.

The membership of Britain's three largest unions, the T.G.W.U., the A.U.E.F.W., and the N.U.G.M.W. overlaps, particularly in the engineering and related industries. It was, perhaps, this overlapping which prompted the N.U.G.M.W. to suggest in 1966 that an amalgamation of the three largest unions would solve a number of problems of industrial relations, and would make it possible to create a single union in a considerable number of factories. Commenting on this proposal, the N.U.G.M.W. said in its evidence to the Royal Commission on Trade Unions and Employers' Associations:

'We are under no illusions about the enormity of the task of securing such an amalgamation. On the assumption of agreement on objectives the harmonization of all the elements which now differ will require several years of painstaking negotiations and work. Given the will for structural reform on the part of the three unions, we believe that the effort can be successful. Failure would mean the indefinite postponement of any prospect for radical reform of the structure of British trade unionism.'

White-collar Unionism

The white-collar unions represent the fastest growing section of the British trade union movement. They have been successful not only in organizing a rising proportion of the total number of white-collar employees but in addition they have been able to recruit from an expanding white-collar labour force. Their growth, however, in recent years is more attributable to the expansion of the white-collar labour force than to any marked increase in the density of trade union membership.

Industrial employees in the middle of the last century consisted almost entirely of manual workers. It has been estimated that in 1851 less than 1 per cent of industrial employees were clerical workers. Technicians at that time were almost non-existent. At the present time, however, white-collar employees in administrative, technical, and clerical occupations represent about a quarter of all industrial employees, and in some industries the proportion is even higher. Moreover, in all industries it is growing from year to year. In addition, the non-industrial services, in which white-collar workers predominate, have also grown considerably. They include national and local government service, banking, insurance, advertising, and entertainment.

White-collar employees can be divided for trade union purposes into certain broad categories. First there are the administrative and clerical employees. There are a number of unions primarily concerned in this field. By far the best organized section are the administrative and clerical workers in public services, including the Civil Service, local government, and the nationalized industries.

The largest union is the National and Local Government Officers' Association with approximately 350,000 members. It has grown very rapidly in recent years. Mr David Lockwood in his book *The Black Coated Worker* recalls that after the First World War in 1921 NALGO organized only about one-third of local government clerks. By 1951 this proportion had risen to about 90 per cent. Today NALGO is a strong and very effective trade union. After much internal controversy it decided eventually in the 1960s to affiliate to the Trades Union Congress.*

The administrative and clerical workers in the Civil Service are

* For a full and informative account of NALGO see *White-collar Union: Sixty Years of NALGO* by Alec Spoor, published by Heinemann, 1967 (70s.).

also well organized in trade unions. The largest union is the Civil Service Clerical Association with about 150,000 members, the majority of whom are women. There are also other well-organized Civil Service unions catering for higher-grade staff. Separate unions also exist in a number of departments of Government service. They include the Inland Revenue Staff Federation, the Ministry of Labour Staff Association, and a number of unions in the Post Office. Both the Union of Post Office Workers and the Post Office Engineering Union include a number of white-collar employees.

In the nationalized industries by far the largest white-collar union is the Transport Salaried Staffs' Association with about 75,000 members. Its base is among administrative and clerical workers on the railways. It has a very high density of trade union membership and is distinguished among white-collar unions by its long and close association with the political Labour movement. It has been affiliated to the Labour Party for many years and a high proportion of its members pay the political levy. It has also had a number of members who have served as trade union sponsored Members of Parliament.

In private industry and commerce the density of trade union membership among clerks is much less than in the public services. The Clerical and Administrative Workers' Union has now more than 75,000 members and it is growing. The number of non-union clerks in private industry and commerce is, however, many times this figure. The National Union of Bank Employees, with nearly 60,000 members, is also growing, and in some of the big banks it now organizes a majority of the staff. The Guild of Insurance Officials, with 15,000 members, is well organized in one or two of the big insurance companies but in the majority it is poorly represented. Outside staff in insurance are organized in a separate union, the National Union of Insurance Workers, with about 37,000 members.

Technical staff have in general shown a greater readiness to organize in trade unions than administrative and clerical staff. In the public services their percentage of membership is at least as high as among clerical staff, and in some branches is even higher. In the Civil Service the Institution of Professional Civil Servants, which, despite its title, is a trade union, organizes a wide variety of professional and technical employees. The Society of Technical Civil Servants has an extremely high density of membership among drawing office grades, and there are also some technicians in the Post Office Engineering Union. In the electricity supply industry the Electrical Power Engineers' Association, with 25,000 members, is a very effective and well-organized union. In broadcasting, television, and film-making there is a high trade union membership among technicians. Most of them, indeed nearly all of them in film-making and in commercial television, are members of the Association of Cinematograph, Television, and Allied Technicians. This Association also has many technicians in the B.B.C. but some of them are also members of the Association of Broadcasting Staff, which extends its cover to all staff employed by the B.B.C.

In private industry many technicians, particularly design staff in the engineering, shipbuilding, and related industries, are members of the 72,000-strong Draughtsmen's and Allied Technicians' Association. The Association of Scientific, Technical, and Managerial Staffs, formed in January 1968 as a result of an amalgamation between the Association of Supervisory Staffs, Executives, and Technicians and the Association of Scientific Workers, also organizes technicians, supervisors, and executive staff in a number of industries and services. Its membership exceeds 80,000.

There are other groups of white-collar workers with a particular skill where there is a tradition of effective trade union organization. They include, for example, journalists, musicians, air crews, and actor. actors.

Finally there is the large body of white-collar employees in the educational service, particularly teachers, where there is a long tradition of semi-professional trade union organization. The National Union of Teachers, though it claims to be primarily a professional body, serves as a trade union for purposes of collective bargaining. It is the largest trade union in Britain not affiliated to the Trades Union Congress.

In the Civil Service, local government, and the nationalized industries there is trade union recognition for white-collar employees. Undoubtedly this is the main reason why white-collar workers in these occupations are generally much better organized than in private industry and commerce. There is little, if any, fear of victimization for trade union activities.

In private industry and commerce the pattern of trade union recognition is very uneven. Even in the industries where some measure of recognition is granted for collective bargaining, there are often many pressures of different kinds on white-collar employees not to join trade unions and, even more, not to become active trade unionists. These pressures may sometimes be open and direct, as when an employer indicates that he is not prepared to recognize a trade union for his white-collar staff and that he would regard with disfavour any attempt to organize his staff employees into a trade union. They may sometimes be much more subtle as, for example, when it is discreetly made known among the staff that persons who become active trade unionists are not likely to be considered for promotion.

In 1964 Britain's principal employers' organization, which was then known as the British Employers' Confederation, conducted an enquiry into the arrangements then in existence among its constituent organizations for dealing with staff trade unions and for collective bargaining on the wages and conditions of staff workers. They reported that of twenty-three employers' organizations which had replied only one was able to state without reservations that trade union representation of staff workers was recognized, that this recognition was on a formal basis, and that agreements covering the rates of pay of staff workers were made at national or company level. A few other employers' organizations indicated that staff unions were recognized to a limited extent, but generally such recognition was limited to a grievance procedure and did not cover the making of agreements. In one other industry unions specifically for staff were excluded from recognition, but recognition had been accorded to a staff section of an appropriate process workers' union.

The British Employers' Confederation stated that the majority of replies to their enquiry indicated either that there was little trade unionism among staff workers or that trade union representation of staff workers was not recognized. The B.E.C. stated, nevertheless, that there was a growing tendency for staff workers to join trade unions and that this was making it increasingly difficult for employers to resist pressure from staff unions for the negotiation of agreements. The B.E.C. went on to state, 'it is recognized that staff unions, because of the type of worker they represent, are generally more articulate, more militant, and more effective than the manual workers' unions and that any development of staff unionism on a major scale will present serious problems for employers.'

37

The British Employers' Confederation suggested that when employers' organizations held discussions with staff unions it would be best if possible to avoid the use of the word 'recognition'. They continued, 'although the development of staff unionism has so far been fairly slow there is a danger in allowing it to spread piecemeal through individual factories or companies without making some attempt to evolve a common policy for the guidance of employers when dealing with the problem. Unexpected concessions to staff unions in one industry or section of an industry might well cause acute embarrassment to employers elsewhere who are also under pressure from the same unions.' The attitude taken by the British Employers' Confederation at the time of this enquiry was severely criticized by a number of trade unions. These criticisms were put to the Royal Commission on Trade Unions and Employers' Associations. In November 1965 the successor to the B.E.C., the C.B.I., issued a Press statement which went some way to acknowledge the growth of trade union membership among staff workers.

Trade Union Federations

In some of Britain's principal industries, notably engineering, printing, and building, the unions have come together to form industrial federations. These federations exist primarily to serve the common interests of the various unions within the one industry for purposes of collective bargaining. In this way British unions seek to obtain for themselves the advantages of industrial unionism without necessarily creating one big industrial union. Unions with members in a number of separate industries do not have to dismember themselves, and craft unions do not have to forfeit the occupational interests of their members.

The authority of these federations varies. The largest, the Confederation of Shipbuilding and Engineering Unions, is also in some ways the one with the least authority. There are nearly forty unions affiliated to the C.S.E.U., but the Confederation has very little power except in relation to central negotiations on national claims affecting all workers in the industry. The Confederation has no power to deal with demarcation disputes.

It is also not customary for the C.S.E.U. to intervene in industrial disputes affecting the members of one particular union. If, however, such a dispute has a bearing on or affects the employment of other trade union members then the union whose members are directly involved in the dispute is required to notify the C.S.E.U. The Confederation then convenes a meeting of representatives of the other affected unions. It has, however, then no further part to play in the proceedings. Its function is merely to act as the convening body for the meeting.

The C.S.E.U. has an annual conference attended by representatives of affiliated unions and delegates from each of the Confederation's district committees. These district committees exist in all the main industrial areas and consist of representatives drawn from each of the local engineering unions.

The Printing and Kindred Trades' Federation covers the unions in printing and publishing. The constituent unions maintain a considerable measure of autonomy on wage negotiations but the Federation deals with regional wage differentials, the principles governing the wages of apprentices, and any general wage movements affecting all workers in the industry. The Printing and Kindred Trades' Federation plays a much more active role than the Confederation of Shipbuilding and Engineering Unions on demarcation disputes and inter-union squabbles. In large printing establishments it is also the practice for the Federation to have its own Federation stewards. The Federation steward is sometimes known as the 'Imperial Father' to distinguish him from the stewards or 'fathers of the chapel' of the individual unions.

The National Federation of Building Trades' Operatives is a more closely integrated Federation than either the C.S.E.U. or the P.K.T.F. It conducts national and local negotiations on wages and conditions through the joint machinery for the building industry; it has its own system of Federation stewards on building sites, and it also provides for the recruitment of building trade workers in 'composite' branches in sparsely populated areas.

Trade union federations of a distinctive kind also exist in the cotton textile industry. A special feature of the unions in this industry is that they are mainly organized 'horizontally' and on a local basis. Thus the weavers and spinners in a local area are usually organized each into a separate local union. These local unions throughout the industry then form part of wider amalgamations. The 'horizontal' amalgamations conduct negotiations with their respective employers' associations, and for the purpose of dealing with matters of general

39

interest to the industry as a whole the unions are represented by the United Textile Factory Workers' Association.

In many other industries where federations do not exist the unions, nevertheless, co-operate with each other for purposes of collective bargaining. They usually meet regularly for this even though they have not created a formal industrial federation. Joint negotiating bodies of this kind are a distinctive feature of British trade union structure.

Trades Union Congress

The Trades Union Congress is the representative national centre of the British trade union movement and consists of affiliated trade unions. Affiliation is a voluntary act: unions are free to affiliate or not to affiliate as they may choose. It has never been the practice of the T.U.C. to canvass for affiliations. The strength of the T.U.C., and the fact that about 90 per cent of all British trade union members are in organizations affiliated to it, is a remarkable testimony to the voluntary support and goodwill enjoyed by the Congress within the trade union movement.

In many other countries in the world the trade union movement is divided along religious or political lines or both. There has never been any such division in Britain. It is not a requirement of affiliation to the T.U.C. that a union should affiliate to the Labour Party or support the Labour Party. Some affiliated unions are, of course, affiliated to the Labour Party but many are not. There is only one large union in Britain which is now not affiliated to the T.U.C. and that is the National Union of Teachers. At the end of 1966 the affiliated membership of the T.U.C. was 8,787,282, enrolled in about 170 unions. Of the total affiliated membership 7,034,127 were men and 1,753,155 were women.

The function of the T.U.C. is to serve the common interests of affiliated trade unions. The criticism is sometimes made that the T.U.C. ought to have more power over its affiliated organizations. Its authority, however, is based upon goodwill and voluntary support. It depends much more upon persuasion than upon compulsion. If each union is to remain democratic it is difficult to see how it would be possible to change this relationship between the T.U.C. and its affiliated organizations. Democracy implies that a union should be answerable, ultimately, not to a central body which stands above it but to its own rank and file. When a union responds to the policies of the T.U.C. it should do so because of a conviction that this is the right thing to do. Even if it maintains its disagreement it may still feel that in the long-term interests of the movement it should voluntarily accept the policy determined by the majority of unions.

It follows from this, therefore, that the power of the T.U.C. can never be described adequately in a formal constitution. When it enjoys the support of its affiliated organizations in a course of action which it is pursuing its power is very considerable. On the other hand, no formal rule can give power to the T.U.C. if the affiliated unions are reluctant to follow its lead.

The main duties of the T.U.C. may be described as follows:

(*a*) To represent to the Government and other national organizations the collective views of the trade union movement on current industrial and economic issues.

(*b*) To keep under review current legislation and to make representations to further the interests of trade unionists.

(*c*) To promote common action between trade unions on issues of mutual interest.

(*d*) To help unions on suitable occasions to secure settlements of disputes in which their members are involved. It is the general practice of the T.U.C. not to interfere in industrial disputes unless they are of such a scale that other trade unionists are likely to become involved. Rule 11 of the T.U.C. sets out the responsibility of the Congress in relation to industrial disputes. It reads:

'The general policy of the General Council shall be that unless requested to do so by the affiliated organization or organizations concerned the Council shall not intervene so long as there is a prospect of whatever difference may exist on the matters in question being amicably settled by means of a machinery of negotiations existing in the trades affected.

'If, however, there is likelihood of negotiations breaking down and creating a situation in which other bodies of workpeople affiliated to Congress might be involved in a stoppage of work, or their wages, hours, and conditions of employment imperilled, the General Council may take the initiative by calling representatives of the organization into consultation and use their influence to effect a just settlement of the difference.'

The T.U.C. is entitled to tender its considered opinion and advice to an organization involved in such a large-scale dispute. If the union or unions refuse the assistance or advice the matter must be reported to the next full Congress.

(e) To uphold the good name of the trade union movement. The T.U.C. has power under its rules to conduct an investigation into the conduct of an affiliated organization if it appears that the activities of the organization are detrimental to the interests of the trade union movement or contrary to the declared principles and policy of Congress. This power is used only with extreme reluctance, except in the most compelling circumstances. The Congress does not interfere in the internal affairs of affiliated unions. It is also traditional to interpret very liberally the words in the rules about activities 'contrary to the declared principles and policy of the Congress'. It is only on the rarest occasions that the Congress have taken the view that it should interfere with a union on the grounds that its policies are contrary to those of the general trade union movement.

(f) To promote the settlement of disputes between affiliated unions. This is a most important function and one on which the unions have vested the Congress with certain powers. When two unions are involved in a dispute, usually about recruitment, it is open to either one of them, failing efforts to reach a settlement by direct discussion, to submit the dispute to the T.U.C. It is then investigated by a committee and a report is made. Frequently the report suggests that further discussions should be held between the two unions and that regard should be paid to certain principles which the T.U.C. may suggest. It is, however, within the power of the T.U.C. to give an award on an issue in dispute and this award must then be accepted by the two organizations. If one of them fails to accept the award it renders itself liable to expulsion from the Congress.

(g) To represent the British trade union movement within the international trade union movement and on other international bodies. The British T.U.C. is affiliated to the International Confederation of Free Trade Unions. The T.U.C. also nominates the workers' representatives for Britain in the International Labour Organization, the specialized agency of the United Nations dealing with labour matters.

(h) To arrange for the registration of local trades councils and to exercise authority over them. A trades council is a local organization of trade union branches. It draws its income mainly from affiliation fees paid by local branches. Local branches are not compelled to affiliate to local trades councils. This is a matter for their own discretion. There are about 530 trades councils in England and Wales registered as local representative bodies by the T.U.C. The functions of trades councils are to provide services to branches on a range of industrial, civic, and educational matters, to assist in improving trade union organization locally, to nominate representatives from the trade union movement to a wide range of local committees and tribunals, and to make more widely known in their area the policies of the T.U.C.

These, then, are the main duties of the Trades Union Congress. Each year the affiliated unions of the T.U.C. meet at an annual congress. Each union is entitled to send delegates roughly proportionate to its membership. The congress is usually attended by about 1,000 delegates. One of the functions of the congress is to elect a General Council of thirty-six members whose task it is to conduct the affairs of the T.U.C. between the annual congresses.

The General Council is elected by the whole congress but on a trade group basis. The engineering, founding, and vehicle building group, for example, is entitled to three members. Each union within this trade group may nominate candidates for these General Council seats. The voting is by the whole congress. Altogether there are twenty trade groups. The distribution of seats on the General Council is not strictly in accordance with the distribution of membership. The idea is to elect a broadly based General Council representative of the varying trade interests in the movement. On the whole the older industries tend to be over-represented on the General Council, and the newer expanding industries under-represented.

Contrary to the public impression the biggest unions, including in particular the T.G.W.U., the A.U.E.F.W., and the N.U.G.M.W., are not over-represented on the General Council in proportion to their size. They are, in fact, under-represented. On the other hand, their command of large votes in the election for the General Council makes it certain that no candidate who is opposed by the big unions is likely to be elected. In practice, however, the big unions are sometimes divided among themselves in their support for rival candidates. It so happens, therefore, that the General Council is not dominated by people from the big unions. A fair number of them are from relatively small unions affiliated to the T.U.C.

The trade group representation on the General Council is as follows:

Mining and quarrying	3
Railways	3
Transport (other than railways)	3
Shipbuilding	1
Engineering, founding, and vehicle building	3
Electricity	1
Iron and steel and minor metal trades	2
Building, woodworking, and furnishing	2
Printing and paper	1
Cotton	1
Textiles (other than cotton)	1
Clothing	1
Leather, boot, and shoe	1
Glass, pottery, chemicals, food, drink, tobacco, brushmaking, and distribution	2
Agriculture	1
Public employees	2
Civil Servants	2
Professional, clerical, and entertainment	1
General workers	3
Women workers	2

The General Council of the T.U.C. usually meets at monthly intervals. It conducts most of its normal work through committees. Committees exist to deal with economic matters, education, organization, international issues, production, social insurance, and industrial welfare.

The General Council presents an annual report to the congress and this is considered by the delegates paragraph by paragraph. It is always a very informative document running into more than 300 pages.

The annual congress also considers motions and amendments submitted by affiliated unions. Each union is entitled to submit two motions. The motions and amendments debated at the congress are more important as a general indication of the trend of trade union opinion rather than as a detailed and considered statement of trade union views on current issues.

44

On important controversial issues it is usual for the congress to take a 'card vote' at the conclusion of debate. This means that the delegates do not vote individually but that each union casts a vote equivalent to the membership on which it is affiliated to the T.U.C. This method is sometimes criticized because it makes no provision for minorities in each union to record their votes. Sometimes too there have been cases where votes have been cast by a leader in apparent defiance of the wishes of the majority of his union's delegation. Such examples, however, are rare and even then there is usually some ground for argument as to whether the individual delegates or the particular union leader is properly carrying out the mandate given by their union's annual conference. Despite the criticism which can be made of it, the 'card vote' system does enable unions to cast their votes in accordance with the mandates given by their respective policy-making bodies, and it gives a voting strength to each union proportionate to its membership.

The T.U.C. and Trade Union Structure

The criticism is sometimes made of the T.U.C. that it should do more to rationalize or streamline the structure of the trade union movement. Critics point out that in some large engineering factories, for example, there may be as many as twenty different unions organizing particular crafts or groups of workers. Would it not be possible, these critics ask, for the T.U.C. to promote the reorganization of the trade union movement on industrial lines?

Undoubtedly there is a need, which is widely acknowledged in the trade union movement, to bring about amalgamation between unions with related trade or industrial interests. On the other hand it is not true that the T.U.C. has been inactive. Major enquiries into trade union structure have been conducted on at least three occasions. The first was in the period 1924 to 1927, the second was in 1943 to 1944, and the third has been from 1962 onwards. Moreover, it should never be overlooked that the T.U.C. has to proceed by persuasion. It cannot compel unions to amalgamate if this is contrary to the wishes of their members.

The 1924 enquiry was initiated by the adoption of a resolution by the T.U.C. endorsing the principle that as far as possible industrial unions should be established. The subsequent enquiry revealed, however, that many sections of the trade union movement were not

45

committed to the principle of industrial unionism. Eventually, after three years of investigation and consultation with affiliated unions, the General Council reported that the 1924 Congress resolution had placed on them an impossible task. They said that the varying structures and methods of working of unions, the differing circumstances in the various trades and industries, and the impossibility of defining industrial boundaries made the general application of any particular scheme impracticable. They stated that any attempt to compel unions to conform to the principle of industrial unionism would destroy all hope of co-operation among the unions. Indeed, said the General Council, it would only create bitterness and strife among the affiliated unions.

The main recommendation to emerge from the enquiry conducted by the T.U.C. between 1924 and 1927 was that unions with closely related industrial interests should enter into joint working arrangements on all industrial matters with a view to joint negotiations on pay and working conditions.

The next major enquiry into trade union structure took place in 1943 and 1944. The report eventually published stated that it remained true as at the time of the earlier enquiry that it was impossible for the T.U.C. to propose schemes of reorganization which involved radical changes in the structure of the movement. They pointed out that as much as they could do was to encourage such tendencies towards better organization as had revealed themselves.

The next major enquiry started in 1962 with the adoption of a resolution urging the movement to adapt its structure to modern conditions. The resolution asked the General Council to examine and report on the possibility of reorganizing the structure both of the T.U.C. and the British trade union movement. Since that time a comprehensive review of trade union structure has been carried out by the General Council.

In 1964 the General Council reported that after giving careful consideration to the arguments for and against industrial unionism they had decided that it would be undesirable to attempt, even over a period of years, to reshape the movement on the lines of one union for each industry. The General Secretary of the T.U.C., Mr George Woodcock, said that the General Council had come firmly to the conclusion that diversity of structure was a characteristic of British trade unionism and always would be. The General Council, he said, saw no hope whatsoever of persuading the present multiplicity and diversity of trade unions into acceptance of a uniform structure, especially an industrial structure.

Partly due to the stimulus of the T.U.C., a number of important mergers have taken place in the movement in recent years. In printing there was a major amalgamation early in 1966 when the National Society of Operative Printers and Assistants and the National Union of Printing, Bookbinding, and Paper Workers merged to form the Society of Graphical and Allied Trades. Somewhat earlier, the National Graphical Association was formed from the amalgamation of two unions of skilled workers in the printing industry. Subsequently, the Association of Correctors of the Press and the National Union of Press Telegraphists merged with the National Graphical Association. In engineering and shipbuilding the engineers and foundry workers have amalgamated to form the A.U.E.F.W. The boilermakers, ship-wrights, and blacksmiths have merged to form one union, and the sheet metal workers and the heating and domestic engineers have amalgamated.

In 1962 the T.U.C. had 182 unions affiliated to it. Between 1962 and 1966 there were seven new affiliations, but the total number of affiliated unions fell to 170. This, in effect, was a reduction of 19 from mergers of various kinds. Several of these mergers were facilitated by the introduction in 1964 of new legislation, the Trade Union (Amalgamations) Act, which eased considerably the legal requirements for amalgamations and transfer of engagements. This new legislation was introduced as a direct result of representations made to the Government by the T.U.C.

The General Council of the T.U.C. are continuing to consult with affiliated unions with a view to promoting mergers between organizations with related trade or industrial interests. No less than twenty-four conferences for this purpose were held between March 1964 and the summer of 1966. Undoubtedly this process of structural change will continue in the trade union movement within the next few years, probably at an accelerated pace.

Employers and Employers' Organizations

Employers' organizations exist both for collective bargaining with trade unions and for mutual consultation and representation on a wide range of economic and trade matters. Moreover, it must not be overlooked, as Professor H. A. Clegg has pointed out in the book *The System of Industrial Relations in Great Britain*, that an employer – at least in a public or private company – is already an 'organization' deriving strength from collective resources and collective action. A large firm which is not a member of an employers' association but which recognizes trade unions and engages in collective bargaining cannot, therefore, be likened to a non-unionist among workers. The Government, for example, employs hundreds of thousands of workers and has a highly complex system of collective bargaining. It is not, however, a member of an employers' association.

For many years there were two central employers' organizations in British industry representing respectively the economic and trade interest of employers, and their collective bargaining interests. The first was the Federation of British Industries and the second the British Employers' Confederation. In July 1965 these two bodies, together with the National Association of British Manufacturers, amalgamated to form the Confederation of British Industry. This central body represents not only private employers but also nationalized industries.

The principal objects of the C.B.I. are defined in its Charter. They are:

(*a*) To provide for British industry the means of formulating, making known, and influencing general policy in regard to industrial, economic, fiscal, commercial, labour, social, legal, and technical questions, and to act as a national point of reference for those seeking industry's views.

(*b*) To develop the contribution of British industry to the national economy.

(*c*) To encourage the efficiency and competitive power of British industry, and to provide advice, information, and services to British industry to that end.

No less than 104 national employers' organizations, 150 trade associations, the main nationalized industries, and principal employers who are not members of employers' organizations are today in membership of the C.B.I. The Confederation membership includes 12,600 individual firms. The national employers' organizations in the C.B.I. represent firms employing more than three-quarters of all workers in private industry and transport.

Though employers come together for the purposes of trade representation and collective bargaining they tend in general to be far more insistent on their individual autonomy than workers in a trade union or even the unions within the T.U.C. The C.B.I. is required by its constitution not to do anything in pursuance of its objects which would interfere with any of its members in the conduct or management of their own affairs, or which would be inconsistent with the retention by members of their complete autonomy and independence of action.

Like the T.U.C., the C.B.I. is not directly responsible for the conduct of industrial negotiations at industry level. Its job is to formulate general policy on behalf of employers, and to express to the Government, the T.U.C., and the public at large the collective views of employers on current problems.

The control of the C.B.I. is in the hands of a Council with 400 members, representative of employers' organizations, trade associations, a number of individual firms, and the Confederation's regional councils. In matters of industrial relations, however, the important committee of the C.B.I. is the Labour and Social Affairs Committee, which has responsibility for all areas affecting relations between employers and employees. It has about 130 members. The 130 members are drawn from nominees of each national employers' organization, together with members appointed by the General Purposes Committee as well as the Economic Committee of the Confederation. The nationalized industries and some of the large individual non-federated firms are also represented on the Committee.

The Labour and Social Affairs Committee has a number of subcommittees dealing with such matters as industrial relations, wages and conditions of employment, vocational training, social insurance, safety, health, and welfare, and international organization.

The policy of the C.B.I. is formulated as a result of extensive consultation with the various representative employers' organizations. In addition, the staff, and particularly the principal officers of the Confederation, have the task of preparing papers, initiating consultation, and helping to guide the thinking of the constituent organizations on new issues as they emerge. The C.B.I. does not have the large-scale and publicly staged formal debates and card votes which are a feature of the trade union movement. In the main the policy of the Confederation and the constituent organizations is moulded and developed in private discussion, and depends much more on consultation and mutual accommodation than on formal debates and votes.

In its evidence to the Royal Commission on Trade Unions and Employers' Associations, the C.B.I. said that one of its major services was to supply to constituent employers' organizations detailed information about negotiations throughout manufacturing and service industries, and analyses of trends in wages, earnings, hours, holidays, and other conditions of employment. The C.B.I. said that confidential information about these matters was freely supplied by member organizations for distribution to other member organizations. Each year the Confederation issues about 250 circulars based on this information and on information about industries not in membership of the Confederation.

Just as the T.U.C. nominates the workers' delegates and advisers to the International Labour Organization, so the C.B.I. is accepted as the representative organization of employers in the United Kingdom. The Confederation also plays a part in the International Organization of Employers. The C.B.I. is also represented with the T.U.C. on a number of consultative committees established by the Government. They are represented, for example, on the National Economic Development Council and the Minister of Labour's National Joint Advisory Council.

The income of the C.B.I. is derived from its constituent organizations and member firms. Work is progressing on a single comprehensive scale applicable both to employers' organizations and to trade associations.

The C.B.I. is not a collective bargaining agent. Collective bargaining is undertaken either by employers' associations at industry level or by individual non-federated firms. The employers' associations range from the largest, the Engineering Employers' Federation, covering firms with about 2 million wage-earners, to small organizations covering firms with only a few thousand wage-earners. Many employers' associations originally came into existence and developed as defensive organizations against the spread of trade unions, trade union claims or strike action. More recently, however, they have developed other and wider functions. They are still primarily collective bargaining agencies but they now provide information, advice, and services on training, safety, productivity, and other matters of common interest.

The C.B.I. evidence to the Royal Commission on Trade Unions and Employers' Associations stated:

'Those persons actively engaged now in employers' organizations' work certainly are not conscious of taking part in a defensive exercise. They regard their tasks as the operation of machinery which is essential to the preservation of industrial peace, and the provision of services which are best organized on an industry rather than a company basis. The philosophy behind employers' organizations is that of providing machinery which encourages decisions in the long-term interests of the industry and the nation as a whole rather than the short-term interest of any side, section or individual company.'

In collective bargaining it is the task of most of the employers' associations not only to help to determine wages and conditions by central negotiations but also to play an active role within the negotiating procedure for resolving grievances. Many industries have procedure agreements which provide for negotiations between local officials of the employers' associations and the trade unions when no agreement has been reached on a grievance within a particular factory. Officials of employers' associations also find themselves in regular informal contact with union officials on a wide range of issues and problems in which there is a mutual interest.

Individual firms look to their employers' associations for advice and guidance on many aspects of industrial relations. This may include the interpretation of collective agreements, the operation of schemes for payment-by-results, the effective use of manpower, redundancy arrangements, and the implementation of statutory requirements under, for example, the Factories Acts, the Offices, Shops, and Railway Premises Act, the Contracts of Employment Act, the Redundancy Payments Act, and the Industrial Training Act.

To help them in providing this advice and guidance many employers' associations collect statistics and other information on industrial relations. They often also collect information on wages and earnings to assist them in central and local negotiations with unions.

Some Employers' Associations

In the following paragraphs a brief outline is given of some of the principal employers' organizations.

The *National Federation of Building Trades' Employers* comprises not only general contractors but also sub-contractors and speculative house builders employing building labour. There are about 16,000 full members, including nearly all the larger firms in the industry. Constituent firms in the Federation employ about two-thirds of the workers in the industry. There are also a number of associates and information members of the Federation. They are building firms not eligible for ordinary membership. They include large industrial and commercial undertakings with their own building departments, local authorities, and public corporations.

The Federation has a regional structure. There are ten regional Federations and over 260 local associations. There are also a number of bodies which are affiliated to the Federation but which deal with a specific section of industry. They include, for example, the Federation of Registered Housebuilders and the National Federation of Plastering Contractors.

The main tasks of the National Federation are to represent the employers in the central collective bargaining machinery for the industry, to negotiate with such bodies as the Royal Institute of British Architects and the Royal Institute of Chartered Surveyors on standard forms of contract, to represent employers in the education and training boards for the industry, and to provide a technical enquiry service to members.

The *Engineering Employers' Federation* is Britain's largest employers' organization engaged in collective bargaining with trade unions. The Federation embraces thirty-nine local associations and covers about 4,500 establishments employing more than 2 million workers. Many non-federated firms follow the agreements and practices of the Federation and so do many firms in other industries employing engineering maintenance craftsmen. Altogether it is estimated that the agreements made by the Engineering Employers' Federation are likely to affect, directly or indirectly, the wages and conditions of more than 3 million workpeople.

The Federation negotiates with trade unions not only on the wages and conditions of manual workers but also on those of white-collar staff employees. A number of white-collar unions are recognized for this purpose, including the Draughtsmen's and Allied Technicians' Association, the Clerical and Administrative Workers' Union, the Association of Scientific, Technical, and Managerial Staffs, and the clerical sections of the two general workers' unions.

Each of the local associations of the Engineering Employers' Federation enjoys a measure of autonomy, but they are required not to make local agreements which conflict with the terms of national agreements. The local associations employ a considerable number of negotiators who conduct negotiations with the unions at factory level and local level.

The Engineering Employers' Federation conducts central negotiations with the Confederation of Shipbuilding and Engineering Unions on minimum wages and conditions for the industry. The Federation also has negotiating procedure agreements with the various engineering unions for the discussion of grievances which arise at factory level. This procedure, known as provisions for avoiding disputes, lays down that issues must first be discussed at factory level; if there is no settlement the grievance can then be discussed at local level. If there is still no settlement it can then be referred for central discussion between the Engineering Employers' Federation and the appropriate union. Strikes and lockouts are permitted only when this procedure of negotiation has been exhausted.

Most of the grievances which are pursued through this procedure are resolved at works level. Even when there is no settlement in negotiations at factory level and the claim is pursued for further negotiations it frequently happens that eventually it is referred back for further discussions at factory level. It is the experience of both employers and the unions that it is usually easier to reach a settlement in discussions at factory level than at later stages in the procedure. The opportunity for flexibility is greater at factory level than elsewhere. Once a grievance is taken to the later stages of the procedure, consideration has always to be given to the implications for other factories of any possible settlements made in the factory where the grievance arose.

In addition to its collective bargaining functions the Engineering Employers' Federation represents the interests of employers in the industry in consultation with Government departments and other public bodies. The Federation also provides an extensive advisory service to federated firms on all problems directly related to labour relations and labour legislation. The Federation also represents employers in the bodies concerned with industrial training and apprenticeship.

In the iron and steel industry certain changes are being made with the introduction of public ownership. The British Steel Corporation, which is responsible for the nationalized sector, has, however, given assurances to the T.U.C. that the collective bargaining machinery and agreements which existed under private ownership will be maintained until they are renegotiated by the unions.

As an experiment in the new nationalized sector of iron and steel, provision is being made for the appointment of part-time members, drawn from among steel workers, to the boards of the new controlling groups.

The private employers in the iron and steel industry had a closely knit and integrated structure extending over a wide field of common interests. Iron and steel firms were members of ten conferences or trade associations concerned with the manufacture of particular iron or steel products. These conferences formed part of the *British Iron and Steel Federation.* The Federation provided machinery for discussing and formulating policy on behalf of firms in the industry, and acted as spokesman for the industry in discussions with the Government and other bodies. The Federation had a staff of about 350 and undertook a wide range of functions. It also performed certain common trading services for the industry and had established several commercial companies for this purpose.

There are ten separately consituted employers' associations responsible for the negotiation of wages and conditions of employment in the industry. These associations constitute themselves into the central council of the *Iron and Steel Employers' Association.* The central council does not itself negotiate with the unions but it provides for the exchange of views and experience between employers in the industry and for the discussion and co-ordination of policy.

An interesting feature of the iron and steel industry is that for the majority of employers and workpeople there are no written negotiating procedure agreements. Nevertheless, there are long-established negotiating arrangements in the industry and nearly all the workpeople are members of their appropriate unions.

The *British Federation of Master Printers* has over 4,000 member firms covering the whole of the general printing industry, excluding newspaper production, and employing approximately 150,000 production workers. The Federation acts not only as a collective bargaining body but also as a commercial trade association. It deals with labour matters, legislation, costing, education and training, and technical developments.

Newspaper production is covered by separate employers' organizations. The Newspaper Society, whose members employ about 35,000 workers, is concerned with morning, evening, and weekly newspapers in the provinces of England and Wales, and London suburban weekly newspapers. Newspaper employers responsible for national morning, evening, and Sunday newspapers are members of a separate Newspaper Proprietors' Association. There are also separate daily and weekly newspaper employers' organizations in Scotland.

3: Collective Bargaining

By collective bargaining is meant the settlement of wages and conditions of employment by means of a bargain reached between employers or organizations of employers and trade unions. Collective bargaining can be contrasted with both individual bargaining and the regulation by the State of terms and conditions of employment.

In individual bargaining, which was normal in the industrial system before the development of trade unionism and is still the practice where there is no trade union organization, the terms and conditions of employment are settled by individual negotiations between employer and worker. This is a bargain struck between two people who are in a grossly unequal position. The employer is economically very much stronger than the individual worker. When there are more unemployed workers than available jobs the worker has little alternative, in the absence of collective bargaining arrangements, but to accept the terms and conditions offered by the employer.

Even now there are millions of workers who probably have the impression that their wages are settled by individual bargaining. They may decide to take a job following a discussion with a supervisor or personnel manager in which there is some haggling about the rate of payment. Nevertheless, the terms which are eventually decided upon will have been materially influenced by the standards already established for similar workpeople. These basic standards, certainly in nearly all manufacturing industries, are determined by collective bargaining and not by individual bargaining.

There are few examples of the regulation of wages and conditions by the unilateral decision of the State. Perhaps the best example of all is provided by the armed services. There is no provision for soldiers, sailors, and airmen to participate in any way in the process of wage determination; nor are the wages of men in the armed forces settled by independent arbitration. The responsibility is one which rests exclusively on the Government of the day, subject, of course, to parliamentary approval.

There are certain other groups of people in British employment whose rights of collective bargaining are circumscribed, but who also have no rights of individual bargaining. The main influence in determining their pay and conditions is that of the Government or other public authority. The police, for example, are in this category, though even they have rather more opportunity to influence the process of wage determination than do the men in the armed services. Members of the police force are prohibited, under the Police Act, 1964, from joining a trade union. They have, however, elected representation on the Police Federations and the Police Council for Great Britain.

Even though there are very few examples of the determination of wages and conditions exclusively by the State it is the long-established practice in Britain for the State to foster the development of collective bargaining. There are today millions of workers employed in occupations where collective bargaining arrangements have been deliberately encouraged and, in some cases, established by the State.

It has been estimated that more than 18 million employees are covered by voluntary collective bargaining arrangements or by statutory wage-fixing machinery. This leaves 5 million employed persons who are outside these arrangements. They include about 3 million non-manual workers, almost all of whom are employed by private employers, and 2 million manual workers. One of the larger groups of manual workers who are not covered by collective bargaining arrangements are those employed in domestic service.

The number of joint negotiating bodies for collective bargaining purposes at national, regional, and workplace level runs into many thousands. According to the Ministry of Labour there are more than 500 pieces of negotiating machinery at national level for manual workers alone, including statutory wage-fixing bodies. Beneath these national bodies there is a wide variety of joint committees covering particular sections of industry, localities, and individual workplaces.

Recognition

Before collective bargaining can take place each side must recognize the other for negotiating purposes. This rarely presents any difficulty to employers because no trade union is likely to refuse recognition to an employer if it wishes to make an agreement with him. The same cannot be said, however, in reverse. There are many employers who, at various times, have disliked the idea of negotiating with trade unions and have resisted or continue to resist recognition for this purpose. There are others who, though they may grant formal recognition, seek to limit the scope of the subjects on which they are prepared to negotiate. From the point of view of the unions, recognition for negotiating purposes is fundamental for their activities.

There is no legal requirement in Britain for an employer to bargain collectively with his employees. There are, however, a number of authoritative international declarations, which have been confirmed by the United Kingdom, which uphold the right to organize and to bargain collectively. There is no doubt, therefore, that short of legal enforcement it is nevertheless the declared national policy of Britain, confirmed by successive Governments, both Labour and Conservative, to uphold the right of association and the right of collective bargaining.

The two main declarations of the International Labour Organization on the right to organize and to bargain collectively are Conventions 87 and 98. The United Kingdom has ratified both these Conventions. It is a requirement of the constitution of the I.L.O. that member states which ratify a Convention have a binding obligation to apply it. Convention 87, which was adopted in 1948 and ratified by the United Kingdom in the following year, provides 'that workers and employers without distinction whatsoever, shall have the right to establish and, subject only to the rules of the organization concerned, to join organizations of their own choosing without previous authorization'. The Convention also insists that workers' and employers' organizations should have the right to draw up their own constitutions, to elect their own representatives in freedom, and to formulate their own policies. Public authorities are required to refrain from any interference which would restrict this right or impede its lawful exercise. Convention 98 provides 'that workers shall enjoy adequate protection against acts of anti-union discrimination in respect of their employment'.

The right to form and join trade unions is also contained in the Universal Declaration of Human Rights which was adopted by the United Nations in 1948 with the support of the United Kingdom.

The right to organize and to bargain collectively is also confirmed in the European Social Charter, which was signed by member countries in 1961 and ratified by the United Kingdom in 1962. One of the articles of the Charter requires member states to undertake to promote joint consultation and machinery for collective bargaining.

In their evidence to the Royal Commission on Trade Unions and Employers' Associations a number of unions submitted suggestions on how these social rights could be protected by law. So far, however, the majority view in Britain has been that general legislation to enforce the right to organize and to bargain collectively might have more disadvantages than advantages. An employer can be compelled to send a representative to a negotiating table but there is no law which can compel negotiators to negotiate with goodwill. Furthermore, if recognition were to be compelled by law there would presumably have to be some requirement that the workpeople concerned had indicated their desire to be represented by a union. Difficulty might then arise about the proportion of workpeople who would have to belong to a trade union before collective bargaining rights could be enforced. Would it have to be a simple majority or would, say, only 30 per cent or 40 per cent be sufficient?

Another difficulty which would be likely to arise concerns the determination of the unit of employment for collective bargaining purposes. Should, for example, a group of toolmakers in a factory be able to demand collective bargaining rights for the toolroom alone, even though they may represent less than 10 per cent of the total labour force in the factory? Problems of this kind, arising from rival claims for craft, occupational or industrial identity, could result in many legal difficulties. Difficulties might also arise in the many establishments where workers, even in the same occupation, are organized in different unions. Would each union be able to insist on negotiating rights or only the union with majority membership?

The Ministry of Labour in their evidence to the Royal Commission said that probably the chief difficulty in making recognition compulsory would arise from the present structure of the trade union movement. It would, they pointed out, be undesirable to encourage further fragmentation by setting up procedures which would encourage unions to seek recognition as representatives of workers who were already covered by collective bargaining machinery or which, on the other hand, would hamper all change and perpetuate the present multiplicity of unions.

The official T.U.C. view is opposed to the legal enforcement of the right to bargain collectively. According to the T.U.C., trade unions in Britain have succeeded largely through their own efforts in strengthening their organization and in obtaining recognition from employers. This, in its view, is an extremely important factor sustaining their strength and independence. Trade unions, say the T.U.C., have not been given legal privileges but instead have fought for what they have achieved. If their strength had been based on legal privilege and their organization had been sustained and strengthened by Government action it might well be logical to argue that the Government had the right at any time to take away or amend trade union functions, including the right of collective bargaining. This the T.U.C. would resist.

Negotiating Rights

In Britain, in comparison with many other countries, the negotiating procedure agreements between employers and unions are fairly narrow in scope. They provide usually for negotiations on wages, hours of work, length of holidays, and certain other standard conditions of employment, but there are a number of issues of concern to workpeople which, by custom or explicit provision, are excluded. Thus, for example, many unions had to fight vigorously to establish a right to discuss and to negotiate on redundancy arrangements. Many employers felt – and some still do feel – that the hiring and discharge of workers according to the economic circumstances of their enterprise was or is, in principle, a managerial right not subject to negotiation.

In the engineering industry there is a long tradition of disputes about the scope of collective bargaining and, in particular, about managerial prerogatives. A very big dispute on this issue was fought after the First World War. The engineering unions were seeking to establish the right to control to some extent overtime working at a time when thousands of their members were unemployed. The employers insisted that it was for the management of each establishment to decide whether overtime working was necessary. The dispute ended in defeat for the unions. The negotiating procedure agreement between the Engineering Employers' Federation and the workshop unions in the industry contains as its first 'general principle'; 'The employers have the right to manage their establishments and the trade unions have the right to exercise their functions.'

Differences of view have also emerged at various times in a number of industries about apprenticeship and other training arrangements. Some employers have held that they alone should determine the proportion of apprentices to journeymen and whether forms of training other than apprenticeship should be introduced. Some craft unions, on the other hand, have sought to control unilaterally the proportion of apprentices to journeymen and have resisted any kind of adult training scheme. The attitude of trade unions in this connection has not always been as selfish as it might at first sight appear. Unions have been concerned at the low standard of training undertaken by some employers and the readiness of some firms to employ apprentices or learners as cheap labour.

Agreements concerning recruitment and training exist in a considerable number of industries. More than 100 such national agreements are known to the Ministry of Labour. Most of these agreements are concerned with apprenticeship or learnerships for young workers.

The Industrial Training Act, 1964, has encouraged joint consultation and bargaining between employers and trade unions on the subject of industrial training. The Act empowers the Minister of Labour to set up industrial training boards charged with the responsibility of training an adequate number of persons, both in quantity and quality, for the industries for which they are responsible. The boards can impose a levy on employers and make grants to those employers whose training courses are satisfactory.

It is one of the complaints of the trade union movement that negotiating procedure agreements in Britain are often unnecessarily narrow in scope and one-sided in operation. Employers, say the unions, are prepared to negotiate on such basic issues as wages, piecework prices, and hours of work, but are much less ready to enter into negotiations on other questions which can, nevertheless, give rise to industrial disputes. Employers are sometimes reluctant to negotiate on, for example, the manning of machines, apprenticeship ratios, occupational pension schemes or redundancy arrangements. Certainly in recent years there have been a considerable number of disputes about redundancy which might have been avoided by earlier consultation and negotiation.

The trade union allegation that negotiating procedure agreements are often one-sided arises from the fact that under many of these agreements workers who want a change to which employers object are expected to go without until the procedure is exhausted. In other words, there is no change of conditions until agreement is reached. In contrast, employers are empowered under certain procedure agreements to introduce changes unilaterally. If the workers object they are expected to invoke the negotiating machinery but in the meanwhile the change in conditions continues. The previous conditions can be restored only by agreement.

Some employers, in reply to this allegation, point out that if industrial efficiency is to be promoted it is unreasonable to expect them always to engage in negotiations before changes are introduced. If new and more efficient machinery is to be brought into a factory it might not always be possible to enter into prior negotiations and to reach agreement with the workers on every problem that might arise.

Negotiating Machinery

The T.U.C. has divided the system of wage and salary determination for Britain's 23 million employees into five main categories. They are as follows:

(a) National machinery making the main agreement on an industry basis, which is closely adhered to at company and local level

7 million employees

(b) Wages Councils   4 million employees

(c) National machinery making the main agreement, but coupled with bargaining within a company which has a big influence on actual earnings   6 million employees

(d) Company machinery making the main agreement

1 million employees

(e) Employees not covered by any joint negotiating machinery

5 million employees

The first category covers virtually the whole of the public sector, including national and local government, educational and health services, the nationalized industries, shipping, and retail co-operative employment. Category (c) includes the engineering industry, shipbuilding, and iron and steel. Nearly half the workers in this category are employed on payment-by-results systems. Category (*d*) includes a number of large companies with their own collective bargaining arrangements. They include, for example, Ford, Vauxhall, and I.C.I.

Most workers in British industry are covered by voluntary collective bargaining arrangements. In some industries the tradition of voluntary collective bargaining goes back for 100 years or more. Nowadays it is customary for national collective bargaining to establish minimum or standard wages and conditions. These are supplemented in industries employing about 6 million workers, as shown in the T.U.C. table above, by negotiations at plant level.

In some industries, notably engineering, shipbuilding, and iron and steel, voluntary collective bargaining arrangements developed between employers and unions with hardly any Government intervention or encouragement. In certain other industries the development of voluntary collective bargaining arrangements was encouraged by the reports of a committee, known as the Whitley Committee, on the relations between employers and employed. This Committee was set up during the First World War and, in all, made five reports. It recommended that Joint Industrial Councils should be established to develop the system of collective bargaining. The Committee urged that in each industry there should be machinery for the regular consideration of matters affecting the progress and well-being of the trade from the point of view of all those engaged in it, so far as this was consistent with the general interest of the community. The Committee also urged that 'a permanent improvement in the relations between employers and employed must be founded upon something other than a cash basis. What is wanted is that the workpeople should have a greater opportunity of participating in the discussion about and adjustment of those parts of industry by which they are most affected'.

Following the publication of these recommendations the Ministry of Labour assisted a number of industries to set up Joint Industrial Councils. The Ministry also drew up a model constitution for such Councils. In some industries, however, where voluntary collective bargaining arrangements were already well established, Joint Industrial Councils on the lines advocated by the Whitley Committee were not set up. Between the beginning of 1918 and the end of 1921 over seventy Joint Industrial Councils were established and a number of other committees of a less formal character were also set up. Some of these Councils and committees went out of existence, but by 1938 there were still forty-five of them in operation. During the Second World War further Joint Industrial Councils were established and there are now about 200 in existence.

In each of the main nationalized industries a statutory obligation has been placed on the Boards responsible for operating the industries to enter into consultation with the workers' organizations regarding the establishment and maintenance of joint machinery for the settlement of terms and conditions of employment, and for joint consultation on matters of common interest. Collective bargaining and joint consultative machinery exists in all the nationalized industries.

Fair Wages Resolution

The operation of the Fair Wages Resolution of the House of Commons also helps to encourage collective bargaining and the observance of collective agreements in industry. The principle of the Fair Wages Resolution is that Government contractors should observe terms and conditions of employment for their employees no less favourable than those established by collective bargaining for the particular trade or industry concerned. The first such Resolution was passed in 1891 and the current one was passed in 1946. The current Resolution lists five main requirements:

1. The contractor is required to observe recognized terms and conditions established for the trade or industry concerned. In the absence of such established conditions the terms and conditions must be not less favourable than the general level of wages, hours, and conditions observed by other employers whose general circumstances in the trade or industry in which the contractor is engaged are similar.

2. The contractor is required to observe 'fair' conditions of work as well as 'fair' wages, and to observe them for all persons employed by him in every factory, workshop or place where the contract is being executed. Moreover, the contractor must, before being invited to tender, give an assurance that to the best of his knowledge he has complied with the general conditions of the Fair Wages Resolution for at least the previous three months.

64

3. The contractor is required to recognize the freedom of his workers to be members of trade unions.

4. The contractor is responsible for the observance of the Resolution by any sub-contractors who may be employed on the contract.

5. Any dispute as to whether or not fair wages are being paid is to be reported to the Minister of Labour and, if not disposed of by negotiation or conciliation, is to be referred to arbitration.

The principle of the Fair Wages Resolution of the House of Commons has been widely extended and embodied not only in Government contracts but in many Acts of Parliament which provide financial assistance to other bodies or industries. The Government has also recommended local authorities to embody the principle of the Fair Wages Resolution in their contracts. Among the Acts of Parliament embodying the principle are the Road Haulage Wages Act, 1938; the Television Act, 1954; the Atomic Energy Authority Act, 1954; the Sugar Act, 1956; the Housing Act, 1957; the Civil Aviation (Licensing) Act, 1960; the Road Traffic Act, 1960; and the Films Act, 1960.

Wages Councils

The main statutory provision for the establishment of collective bargaining in industries where voluntary arrangements have not been established on a satisfactory basis is contained in the Wages Councils Act, passed in 1959. It consolidated earlier legislation providing for statutory wage-regulating machinery. The first such legislation was the Trade Boards Act, 1909, which was introduced following the widespread expression of public concern about wages and conditions in a number of 'sweated' industries. At the outset, attention was focused on four trades only, namely tailoring, paper-box making, chain-making, and machine-made lace and net finishing. The Trade Boards established under the Act were charged with fixing minimum time rates of wages, and a wages inspectorate was set up to enforce the minimum rates.

The principle of statutory wage regulation was extended in a new Trade Boards Act passed in 1918. This empowered the Minister of Labour to set up a Trade Board in a section of industry if, having regard to the level of wages, he considered that no adequate machinery existed for the effective regulation of wages. In the years between the two wars approximately fifty Trade Boards were established covering about 1½ million workers. Similar legislation was also introduced for statutory wage regulation in agriculture. Separate Agricultural Wages Boards were set up for England and Wales and for Scotland.

Further legislation was introduced in 1945 when the Trade Boards Acts were superseded by a new Wages Councils Act. This was again amended in 1948, and new consolidated legislation was passed in 1959. The underlying purpose of the Wages Councils Act is the same as for the original Trade Boards Act. It is to establish and to encourage collective bargaining in industries where conditions are particularly bad or where the level of organization among employers and workpeople is so low that effective collective bargaining on a voluntary basis is unlikely to be established. Wages Councils today, however, have much wider scope than the original Trade Boards. They can submit proposals not only for minimum time rates of wages but also for piecework rates, overtime rates, lengths of holidays, holiday pay, and guaranteed minimum weekly remuneration.

Proposals made by a Wages Council are submitted to the Minister of Labour. The Minister is not legally obliged to accept a proposal from a Wages Council: he cannot, however, reject or amend it. He must either accept the proposal and make an Order to give effect to it, or, alternatively, he may refer the proposal back, together with his observations, for further consideration by the Council. If the Wages Council, having reconsidered its proposals, decides, nevertheless, to send them back unchanged the Minister has no alternative but to make an Order giving the proposals legal effect.

There are now more than fifty Wages Councils in existence, covering about 3½ million workers. Each Council consists of members in equal numbers, representing employers and workers in the trade or industry covered, together with a number of independent members, one of whom, appointed by the Minister, acts as chairman. Before appointing the members representing respectively employers and workers the Minister is required to consult any existing representative organizations in the industry. The independent members are mainly drawn from among university lecturers and lawyers.

There are a number of main sections of employment where Wages Councils exist, including retail distribution, catering, and clothing manufacture. They also exist in a number of minor industries such as aerated-water manufacture, boot- and floor-polish manufacture, sack and bag manufacture, and shirt-making.

The minimum rates and conditions established by Wages Councils are legally enforceable. Workplaces in the various industries covered by Wages Councils are inspected regularly by officials appointed by the Ministry of Labour. If the required minimum conditions are not being observed legal proceedings can be taken against the employer, irrespective of whether or not a complaint has been received. A worker or group of workers may also take legal proceedings for the recovery of arrears of pay.

Under the terms of the Wages Councils Act, 1959, the Minister of Labour can abolish a Wages Council if he is satisfied that adequate machinery for the effective regulation of pay and conditions of employment exists and that this machinery is substantially representative of both sides of the industry concerned. The machinery for collective bargaining must be able not only to produce agreements in the industry but also to ensure that these agreements are observed. If either of these requirements does not exist a Wages Council cannot be abolished by the Minister, no matter how strongly one side may press for it. Only a few Wages Councils have been abolished in the years since the ending of the Second World War.

In most of the industries covered by Wages Councils both employers and workers do not wish to surrender the benefits derived from the statutory machinery. This machinery has obvious advantages to the workers, and it also had advantages to employers who are prepared to observe the statutory minimum conditions. They are protected against unfair competition from more unscrupulous employers who might be prepared to employ 'sweated' labour.

Statutory Provision for Conciliation and Arbitration

Support for the system of collective bargaining in Britain is provided by statutory provisions for conciliation, arbitration, and State enquiry into disputes. Although these provisions are extremely important and are fairly frequently used it is nevertheless the general principle behind them that they should be used only when the two sides of industry have found themselves unable to reach a settlement. In its report on conciliation and arbitration the Whitley Committee stated: 'we desire to emphasize the advisability of a continuance, as far as possible, of the present system whereby industries make their

F   67

own agreements and settle their differences themselves.' This is still a guiding principle for the Ministry of Labour in relation to industrial disputes.

The conciliation service of the Ministry derives its authority from the Conciliation Act, 1896, and the Industrial Courts Act, 1919. When there is a dispute between employers and workers the Minister may 'take such steps as may seem expedient for the purpose of enabling the parties to the difference to meet together, by themselves or their representatives, under the presidency of a chairman mutually agreed upon or nominated by the Minister or by some other person or body, with a view to the amicable settlement of the difference'. Nowadays the conciliation service is staffed by permanent officials of the Ministry. It is rare for the Minister to appoint independent conciliators.

The Ministry has considerable discretion in deciding at what stage and in what manner it will intervene in an industrial dispute for purposes of conciliation. Normally the Ministry satisfies itself that any agreed procedure has been exhausted by the two sides to the dispute before the process of conciliation begins.

There is no legal compulsion on either employers or workers to assist or even to participate in the process of conciliation. The Ministry's officials usually talk separately to both of the parties to the dispute so as to find the essential facts. At a later stage the officials may invite the two parties to meet together under the chairmanship of a conciliation officer of the Ministry. The job of the conciliation service of the Ministry of Labour is not to act as an arbitrator. The conciliation service exists to explore the attitudes of the two sides and to find out whether there is an acceptable basis for a settlement. The Ministry does not accept responsibility for any settlement which may be reached with the aid of the conciliation service. The responsibility for any settlement rests with the employers and the unions concerned.

Each year the conciliation service of the Ministry of Labour is used in more than 400 separate disputes. About half of the disputes concern questions of pay, and nearly a third relate to trade union recognition. Disputes about recognition are the most difficult for the conciliation service. The Ministry recognizes that in a dispute about recognition it cannot, in practice, take up a neutral position, particularly if the employer refuses to recognize a trade union of any kind for purposes of collective bargaining. It is long-established national policy to uphold collective bargaining and the conciliation service is bound, in the circumstances, to appear to the employer as an agent for the union.

The Minister of Labour's powers to provide voluntary arbitration in industrial disputes are derived, like his similar powers of conciliation, from the Conciliation Act, 1896, and the Industrial Courts Act, 1919. The Minister may refer an existing or apprehended trade dispute for settlement by arbitration providing that the parties to the dispute consent to this course of action. If either party refuses to give its consent then arbitration cannot take place. Furthermore, before referring a dispute for voluntary arbitration the Minister must be satisfied that the negotiating machinery in the trade or industry concerned has been fully exhausted without a settlement having been reached.

The Minister may refer a dispute for voluntary arbitration either to an industrial court, an individual arbitrator or a board of arbitration. A board of arbitration consists of one or more persons nominated by the employers and an equal number nominated by or on behalf of the workers involved in the dispute, together with an independent chairman nominated by the Minister.

The Industrial Court was established in 1919 as a permanent arbitration tribunal for industrial disputes. It should be carefully noted, however, that it is *not* a court of law in the generally understood sense. The members of the Court are appointed by the Minister and consist of representatives of employers, representatives of workers, and independent persons.

The Industrial Court has considerable discretion as to the manner in which it conducts its business. The parties to a dispute may or may not be represented by lawyers. In practice most of the cases on behalf of workers are presented by full-time trade union officials and not by lawyers. Although the awards of the Industrial Court are normally not legally binding they are almost invariably accepted by the parties to a dispute.

Machinery for voluntary arbitration, other than that provided by the Industrial Court, exists in a considerable number of industries. In the nationalized industries, for example, it is widely accepted that unresolved claims or grievances should be referred to arbitration as a means of avoiding stoppages of work. Permanent provision for arbitration is made in coal-mining, on the railways, in the Civil Service, and in teaching.

Compulsory arbitration, in the strict sense that all industrial disputes must be referred to arbitration and that strikes and lockouts are illegal, has never been a permanent feature of industrial relations in Britain. Compulsory arbitration did, however, exist between 1940 and 1951 under the Conditions of Employment and National Arbitration Order. This was commonly known as Order 1305. Under the terms of this Order either party to a dispute could report it to the Minister of Labour. The Minister could then refer it for arbitration to a National Arbitration Tribunal. Strikes and lockouts were prohibited unless the Minister failed to act within twenty-one days of the dispute being reported to him. Before referring a dispute to the National Arbitration Tribunal the Minister satisfied himself that the negotiating machinery of the trade or industry in which the dispute existed had been exhausted. Under the terms of Order 1305 all employers were also obliged to observe terms and conditions settled by collective agreement or by arbitration for the trade concerned.

Rather surprisingly Order 1305 lasted for some years after the War. In 1951, however, it was replaced by the Industrial Disputes Order. This provided for compulsory arbitration only in the sense that if a dispute were reported to the Minister and the Minister then referred it to the Industrial Disputes Tribunal the other party to the dispute could not prevent the dispute being heard at the Tribunal and an award being given. The awards of the Tribunal were legally binding upon both parties. The vital difference between the Industrial Disputes Order and the earlier Arbitration Order was that under the Industrial Disputes Order neither a trade union nor an employer was compelled to seek a settlement of a dispute by arbitration. Either party to a dispute could, if it so wished, call a strike or lockout. Strikes and lockouts were not illegal under the Industrial Disputes Order whereas they were in most circumstances illegal under the Arbitration Order.

In 1959 the Industrial Disputes Order was brought to an end. It had always been understood that the Order would continue to exist so long as it was supported by the unions and the employers. In 1959, however, the main employers' organizations indicated that they no longer supported the principle of the Order. They felt that the principle was one-sided in operation. The T.U.C. subsequently asked for the restoration of the arbitration provisions of the Industrial Disputes Order. The Government undertook to examine this request but so far a new Order has not been introduced.

The Government did, however, introduce new legislation after the ending of the Industrial Disputes Order in 1959 to enforce recognized terms and conditions of employment. This provision was contained originally in the Arbitration Order and was continued in the Industrial Disputes Order. A new piece of legislation was introduced – the Terms and Conditions of Employment Act, 1959 – which gave representative organizations of employers or workers the legal right to invoke through the Minister of Labour the adjudication of the Industrial Court on claims for the observance of recognized terms and conditions of employment. By 'recognized terms and conditions' is meant terms and conditions of employment established by agreements or awards for the industry in which the claim is made. The Industrial Court, which hears claims of this kind, is empowered to make an award requiring the employer against whom a claim is made to observe the recognized terms and conditions. This award then has effect as an implied term of the contract of employment and can be enforced in a normal court of law.

To many outside observers arbitration appears to have so many advantages as a method of settling industrial disputes that they are surprised that it is not universally used. It avoids the loss of production and the hardships caused by strikes or lockouts, and it enables the facts of a dispute to be examined dispassionately. Some feel that it encourages an attitude of industrial responsibility on the part of both employers and trade unions. Neither side, it is sometimes suggested, is likely to adopt an utterly unreasonable attitude if its arguments may be submitted ultimately to arbitration.

Despite these apparent advantages arbitration has not commended itself to all sections of British industry as a method of resolving disputes. It has its drawbacks. In the first place, if arbitration is built into the negotiating arrangements for an industry there is less likelihood that the negotiators will feel that the responsibility to reach a settlement rests with themselves. It will be easier for them to shift the responsibility on to the shoulders of the arbitrators. To this extent a built-in provision for arbitration may have the effect of undermining the normal process of negotiation.

Secondly, there are many kinds of dispute which cannot be resolved by reference to existing practice or an existing agreement. In this connection, disputes can be divided into two categories. There are disputes about the interpretation of existing practices or agreements. Disputes of this kind are usually suitable for arbitration. On the other hand, there are disputes which arise from claims for changes in existing agreements or practices. Claims of this kind can rarely be resolved by reference to other agreements. At best an arbitrator can seek to find a middle way or compromise which might be acceptable to both parties or, in certain cases, he may be able to refer to general standards already established in other industries.

The real problem about arbitration on claims for changes in existing agreements and practices is that there is really no universally accepted standard by which an arbitrator can determine how the product of industry should be divided. There are all kinds of views about how much should go to capital development, how much should be paid out as dividends to shareholders, and how much should go as wages and salaries. People have different views on these issues, depending usually upon their basic political philosophy. This, however, is only another way of saying that it is very difficult indeed for any person who has taken a strong interest in public affairs to be genuinely independent and impartial on a claim for a change in existing agreements.

Arbitration may, therefore, be acceptable to the two sides to a dispute as an ultimate means of reaching a compromise, but it is not likely to commend itself to either party as a means of finding a just and permanently acceptable solution to a problem on which they feel very strongly. There are many employers and trade unionists, therefore, particularly in private industry, who may on occasions when all else has failed accept arbitration but who are not prepared to accept it as a normal procedural obligation.

Courts of Enquiry

The Conciliation Act and the Industrial Courts Act also empower the Minister of Labour to enquire into industrial disputes. For this purpose the Minister may appoint a Court of Enquiry or a Committee of Investigation. The formal powers of a Committee of Investigation are rather less than those of a Court of Enquiry.

The purposes of a Court of Enquiry and of a Committee of Investigation are much the same. Their task is to ascertain the facts and the underlying causes of a dispute. The report is then presented to the Minister and serves to inform the Minister, Parliament, and the public about the dispute. Courts of Enquiry and Committees of Investigation are not required to make recommendations in their reports but they often do so. The recommendations sometimes provide a basis upon which a settlement can be reached or upon which further negotiations can take place.

The Minister does not use his power to set up a Court of Enquiry except in major disputes where the national interest is likely to be affected. Courts of Enquiry usually consist of an independent chairman, a person drawn from an employers' organization other than in the industry where the dispute has occurred, and a person drawn from the trade union movement but from a union other than one directly involved in the dispute.

Strikes

A strike is a concerted withdrawal of labour by a group of workers. Its purpose is to induce or compel an employer to do something which he was not prepared to do by negotiations alone. The strike weapon is the ultimate sanction of workers.

It is a mistake to think that good industrial relations can be measured solely by the absence of strikes. Of course, if there are persistent strikes in an establishment or in an industry it is an indication that something is wrong, but the converse does not necessarily hold. The absence of a strike in an establishment or an industry may indicate that there is an absence of trade union organization, an absence of trade union consciousness among workers, an ineffective trade union leadership, or an attitude of servility or docility on the part of many of the workers towards their employers. In an establishment where there is a glaring injustice the readiness of workers to take strike action following abortive negotiations will almost certainly help rather than hinder future good industrial relations.

Since the end of the Second World War Britain has lost on average roughly 3 million working days each year because of strikes. The average number of days lost since 1955 has been considerably higher than the average in the ten-year period 1945–54.

The following table, taken from the evidence of the Ministry of Labour to the Royal Commission on Trade Unions and Employers'

Associations, shows how the strike figures for recent years compare with the figures for earlier periods:

Period	Average number of stoppages per year	Average number of workers involved per year	Average number of working days lost per year
1914–18	814	632,000	5,292,000
1919–21	1,241	2,108,000	49,053,000
1922–32*	479*	395,000*	7,631,000*
1933–39	735	295,000	1,694,000
1940–44	1,491	499,000	1,816,000
1945–54	1,791	545,000	2,073,000
1955–64	2,521	1,116,000	3,889,000

* Excluding 1926, the year of the General Strike and coal-mining dispute, when over 162 million days were lost.

The Ministry of Labour table shows that the number of days lost through strikes in Britain since the end of the Second World War has been more than the average lost during the period 1933–39, but less than during the 1920s, and much less than in the period immediately following the ending of the First World War. The number of stoppages on the other hand, as distinct from the number of working days lost, has risen considerably during the last ten years. Since 1945 there have never been less than 2,000 stoppages of work each year. This is higher than during any previous ten-year period. Thus, the indications are that the number of strikes in Britain has tended to rise, but the total number of days lost through strike action is less than in certain earlier periods in British history.

This contrast between the number of stoppages and the amount of time lost corresponds with the fact that in recent years there has been a growth in the number of unofficial stoppages of short duration, whereas in earlier periods the big stoppages, which resulted in the loss of millions of working days, were called officially by the unions. Even in the last ten years or so most of the big stoppages of work, which have caused the greatest loss of time, have been called officially by the unions. There were, for example, big engineering and ship-building strikes in 1957 and in 1962. In 1959 some $3\frac{1}{2}$ million days were lost because of a strike in the printing industry and in 1962 there was a one-day strike on the railways.

Contrary to a widespread public impression, Britain's strike record compares favourably with that of most other industrial countries.

During the last ten years only Western Germany has lost fewer days through strikes per 1,000 persons employed than Britain. More time has been lost per 1,000 employees in the U.S.A., France, Italy, Japan, India, Australia, Belgium, Canada, Denmark, Ireland, and Finland. There is nothing in the official figures to suggest that industrial unrest in Britain is substantially greater than in other industrial countries.

In recent years the great majority of stoppages of work have been unofficial. This means that they have not received the prior sanction of the executive authority of the union. It is the fact that most strikes in Britain are unofficial that has probably tended to contribute to the public impression that British industry is frequently paralysed by strike action. Unofficial strikes are given prominence by newspapers and blame is invariably attached to the workers involved. Nevertheless, even though a strike is unofficial when it begins, it does not necessarily follow that the workers are acting in a manner which is deplored by the official leadership of the union. The T.U.C. found, for example, in an investigation which they made that in nearly one-half of the so-called unofficial strikes the unions' executive committee subsequently authorized the payment of dispute benefit. There are many examples of strikes which begin unofficially but are subsequently made official by the union concerned. Many trade union executive committees consist mainly of lay members and meet at monthly intervals. It is not always possible for them to give prior approval to strike action, particularly if the strike has arisen because of an immediate worsening or change of conditions.

The terms 'unofficial strike' and 'unconstitutional strike' are sometimes used as though they were synonymous. There is, however, a difference between them. An unofficial strike is one which has not received the support of the union concerned. An unconstitutional strike is one which is called in breach of the negotiating procedural obligations of the union. An unconstitutional strike, in the sense that it is in breach of procedure, is usually an unofficial strike, but an unofficial strike, if it is called after the negotiating procedure has been exhausted, is not unconstitutional.

Strikes are not spread evenly across British industry. There are certain industries with a much higher incidence of strikes than others. The main strike-prone industries are coal-mining, motor-car manufacture, shipbuilding, and port transort. There are a number of special reasons for the frequency of strikes in these industries. In some of them a large proportion of the workers are employed on payment-by-results. Negotiations are constantly taking place about piecework prices for new work. In three of the industries, coal-mining, shipbuilding, and docks, the workers are always likely, by the nature of the work, to be faced by new problems or hazards. In none of these industries is there repetition production each working day under identical conditions.

In each of these industries there is also a tradition of instability. In coal-mining and shipbuilding there have been periods of heavy unemployment. Until the autumn of 1967, when a decasualization scheme was introduced, many of the workers in the docks were employed under schemes which did not identify them with a particular employer. It has yet to be seen what long-term effect decasualization will have on industrial relations in the docks. The casual relationship between employer and worker to some extent remains. In motor-car manufacture there have been periods of slackness in between the longer periods of prosperity. During these periods of slackness workers have been stood off, and this has probably contributed to the feeling among workers that as much as possible should be obtained 'while the going is good'.

When there is an unofficial strike in an establishment it must not necessarily be assumed that the fault lies with the workers who have withdrawn their labour. The fault may, of course, be theirs but there may also be other underlying causes. In some unofficial strikes the workers undoubtedly take precipitate action which is both unnecessary and disruptive of good relations. They may, indeed, have been misled into taking such action by a representative who is able to point to a real grievance but who does not favour seeking redress through the proper channels.

An unofficial strike may, however, indicate that there is something wrong with the union of which the workers are members. It may perhaps be that the local officials or the national leadership have not responded adequately to representations made to them on behalf of the workers. In such a case an unofficial action by the workers may be as much a protest against the inadequacy of the union as it is against the management.

Unofficial action may also be taken because workers feel incensed at changes introduced by the management. As already explained, under many negotiating procedure agreements employers are entitled to introduce certain changes without negotiation. If the workers protest, they are required to continue at work under the changed conditions and, in the meanwhile, to invoke the machinery of negotiations to express their protest and to try to restore the former conditions. Sometimes the change introduced by the management may cause such ill feeling among the workers that they feel that an immediate protest is justified.

An employer may also take other forms of provocative action which contribute to a situation in which workers participate in an unofficial strike. If, for example, an employer victimizes an active trade union representative it is likely that his hostility will be met by protest action from the workers. If the victimization is particularly blatant, as for example the dismissal of a shop steward, immediate strike action is likely to follow.

Finally, unofficial strike action may be taken by workers as a protest against procrastination in negotiations. A negotiating procedure agreement can provide no more than a framework within which negotiations should take place. It cannot ensure that negotiations are conducted with goodwill. There are occasions in which an employer will deliberately use the negotiating procedure as a means of delay. Such tactics are likely to evoke protest action from workers.

It is clear, therefore, that no immediate conclusion can be drawn as to the causes of unofficial strikes. Each particular case has to be examined according to its own circumstances. There is no simple remedy for unofficial strikes. In the final chapter of this book, consideration is given to some of the suggestions which have been put forward for changes in the law to help reduce the number of unofficial strikes.

Workplace Bargaining

A feature of collective bargaining in recent years has been the increasing importance of negotiations and agreements at workplace level. For the most part these agreements are not intended to replace national agreements concluded between employers' associations and trade unions but to supplement them. The T.U.C. estimates that there are now about 6 million workers employed in industries where the main agreement is made nationally but is then supplemented with bargaining at workplace level. This bargaining has a big influence on actual earnings.

The development of bargaining at plant level is undoubtedly connected with the maintenance of near full employment during most of the postwar period. When there is a strong demand for labour, employers are more likely to be persuaded by local trade union representatives to pay higher wages or make other concessions in order to attract more labour. The opportunities for plant bargaining are probably greater in industries where there exists some form of payment-by-results. The negotiations which follow from changes in methods or materials or the introduction of new models inevitably afford the workers' representatives an opportunity to force up earnings.

The largest single group of industries in which the system of factory bargaining is strongly developed is engineering. The Engineering Employers' Federation have described very clearly in their evidence to the Royal Commission on Trade Unions and Employers' Associations how national negotiations are supplemented by factory bargaining. National negotiations, they pointed out, are today reserved largely for the establishment of national minimum time rates for a number of key classes of workers and the establishment of differentials for other classes. National agreements also determine basic conditions of employment, such as the length of the working week; the conditions relating to overtime, night shift, and the operation of shift systems; the duration of and payment for holidays; the guarantee of employment; and certain principles relating to the operation of systems of payment-by-results. National negotiations also take place upon claims for general increases in wages or improvements in the established conditions of employment.

The Engineering Employers' Federation pointed out that in such a wide complex of industries loosely referred to as engineering it would be impracticable to negotiate at national level a standard as distinct from a minimum wage rate for each class of worker. Similarly, it would be impracticable to negotiate at national level lists of standard piecework prices. Negotiations on these questions must, therefore, take place at factory level.

Factory negotiations in engineering are usually concerned with piecework prices or times, payments in lieu of piecework to time workers, merit payments to particular workers or groups of workers, starting and stopping times each day, the actual days to be observed as holidays, rules about clocking on and off, the time of wage pay-

78

ments, details regarding the notification of sickness, offences against factory discipline, and conditions relating to the physical environment.

It is sometimes alleged that the development of factory bargaining to supplement national agreements has been responsible for the increasing gap between minimum rates and actual earnings in industry. This is usually described as 'wage drift'. Actual wage earnings in many factories are sometimes as much as 50 per cent or even higher than the agreed national minimum rates. Moreover, throughout the postwar period earnings in British industry and commerce have been rising substantially faster than output. Since 1950, until the wage standstill was introduced in the summer of 1966, followed by the period of severe restraint, wages and salaries per employee had been rising at an annual rate of about 6 per cent. In contrast, the growth in national productivity over the same period has been less than $2\frac{1}{2}$ per cent.

It must not, however, be automatically assumed that if there were no factory bargaining the problem of wage drift would be solved. If the economy is over-stretched and there is a shortage of labour employers are likely to bid against each other for the workers they require. Factory bargaining, therefore, merely puts in institutionalized form a process which would in any case take place. The causes of inflation are more complex than is suggested by the simple proposition that if wages rise faster than output prices are also bound to rise. Wages may rise because of the pull of aggregate demand. The Government of the day may have failed to relate the total commitments of the economy to the available resources. Trade union pressure for higher wages may, therefore, be more a symptom than a basic cause of inflation. Further, it should not be overlooked that the problem of wage drift is one which is common to all countries in Western Europe where somewhere near full employment has been maintained. Indeed, in comparison with most other industrialized countries in Western Europe, wage rates and wage earnings in Britain have risen rather more modestly. Thus the problem of wage drift is not something peculiar to British industrial relations.

British trade unions do not favour the abandonment of national agreements on minimum wages and conditions. For many years they struggled to achieve industry-wide collective bargaining, and in the main industries they secured this objective in the years before and during the First World War. Industry-wide agreements on minimum wages and conditions proved of considerable advantage to British workers in the interwar period. Unions were able more effectively to resist demands by certain employers for wage reductions or the lengthening of working hours. If there had been no national agreements the bargaining strength of the unions would have been fragmented. They would have had little or no strength to resist pressure for wage reductions or a worsening of conditions in the firms or sections of industry most affected by the depression.

The maintenance of national agreements on minimum rates and conditions during the interwar period was also of advantage to many employers. It protected them against cut-throat competion from other employers who might be prepared to employ labour under 'sweated' conditions.

Productivity Bargaining

During the 1960s a new term, 'productivity bargaining', came into the vocabulary of industrial relations. Productivity bargaining is usually associated with factory or plant bargaining. Its purpose is to promote the efficient use of resources in an establishment, including both capital equipment and labour, and to provide that some share of the rewards from this greater efficiency goes to the workers concerned. Productivity agreements usually provide for increases in pay related to specific alterations in methods of work.

A fuller definition of productivity agreements is provided in the report of the National Board for Prices and Incomes on *Productivity and Pay during the Period of Severe Retraint* (Command 3167). It says that a productivity agreement in strict terms is 'not one in which increases in pay are accompanied by vague promises to increase output. It is one which introduces new standards of work measurement and new methods of control to ensure that the standards are subsequently adhered to'. The National Board for Prices and Incomes in its report carefully distinguished between a true productivity agreement and an agreement relating merely to payment-by-results. It emphasized that a true productivity agreement presupposes careful advance preparation, and more often than not involves the reorganization of management, including possibly the replacement of supervisors, the elimination of charge-hands, extensive training programmes, and the reconstruction of departmental organization to facilitate the introduction of new methods. Thus, productivity agreements exchange a number of improvements in pay and conditions for a series of changes in performance and practice throughout the plant or plants concerned.

When a productivity agreement is being negotiated it is customary for the employer to identify a number of inefficiencies in his plant or organization. He then seeks, with the co-operation of the unions, to remove or overcome these inefficiencies by changes in manning schedules, overtime arrangements, shift working or the employment on different jobs of various categories of labour. In return for this co-operation higher rates of pay are negotiated. A special feature of productivity agreements is that methods of promoting the efficient use of manpower and resources are stipulated more explicitly than in normal collective bargaining agreements.

Although much has been heard recently of the development of productivity bargaining the number of real productivity agreements in British industry is still very limited. The National Board for Prices and Incomes stated that over the six years, 1960-6, probably not more than half a million workers had been affected by them.

Shop Stewards

No account of the process of collective bargaining in Britain, no matter how brief, would be adequate without a reference to the vitally important part played by lay representatives of trade union members at workplace level. These lay representatives exist under various names and titles, but by far the most common, and the one by which they are most generally known, is that of 'shop steward'.

Many unions provide either by rule or by custom for their members to elect at workplace level lay representatives who undertake a fairly wide range of responsibilities. These responsibilities vary to some extent from union to union, but they often include negotiations on immediate problems faced by workers at their workplace, the collection of union subscriptions, the recruitment of non-members, the regular inspection of the membership cards of the existing members, the distribution of notices and other trade union literature, and communication between workpeople collectively and the management. The total number of lay representatives of this kind is not known. It has been variously estimated at between 80,000 and

200,000. Probably the higher of these two figures is the more accurate. Whatever the real figure it is clear that it is almost impossible to exaggerate the importance of shop stewards for the effective functioning of industrial relations in British industry.

It is as workplace bargainers with management that the stewards have their greatest influence. In general their influence tends to be greatest in the establishment where, through their negotiations, they are able to influence the earnings of the men and women they represent. Even, however, where they have no direct influence on earnings, because there is no piecework system or because wages are fixed by negotiations with full-time officials, the stewards are nevertheless able to influence a wide range of other matters of direct interest to the workers. Effective trade unionism today, particularly in manufacturing industry, would be impossible without some system of lay representation at workshop level. Whatever criticism might be made of individual shop stewards there is no doubt that as a group they play an essential role in modern trade unionism and collective bargaining.

The most thorough study of the role of shop stewards in industrial relations, and in collective bargaining in particular, is contained in a research paper prepared by Dr W. E. J. McCarthy for the Royal Commission on Trade Unions and Employers' Associations*. This study found that the most common argument used by stewards to justify grievances and claims was an appeal to some kind of comparison with another individual or group in similar circumstances, or employed on similar work. These arguments about comparability were based on information obtained by shop stewards through various forms of informal and formal contact with other stewards.

Dr McCarthy showed that collective bargaining at workshop level involves the use both by workers and management of a variety of sanctions. The sanction most frequently used by workers is a ban on overtime. Various other forms of sanctions are also employed, including the withdrawal of co-operation on various minor questions, an insistence on the observance of formal rights and customs, the limitation of output and, its most extreme form, a withdrawal of labour.

Similarly, managements also have various kinds of sanctions which they can impose. They can become generally less co-operative and

* Dr. McCarthy is the Royal Commission's Research Director.

demand the rigid observance of existing agreements. They can tighten up on facilities previously enjoyed by shop stewards. Stricter supervision can be enforced and various privileges can be withdrawn. Dr McCarthy in his study concludes that there has now developed a form of workplace bargaining where the parties immediately involved have come to accept that sanctions are a part of the normal background against which day-to-day negotiations take place on the workshop floor. These sanctions, it should be noted, are not provided for in the official negotiating procedure agreements between employers and unions. Nevertheless, they are a reality in many sections of British industry.

A great deal of collective bargaining at workshop level is informal. It results not in written agreements but in understandings which are accepted for the time being both by management and workers. This almost universal reliance on informal arrangements and understandings in shop-floor bargaining, Dr McCarthy suggests, does not arise out of the mutual interests of the two sides but is more a result of their continued conflict and opposition. Employers prefer informal understandings because they are reluctant to establish formal precedents which might then be quoted against them when conditions are less favourable from the workers' point of view. In other words an informal understanding can always be regarded as a temporary arrangement which is likely to last only so long as existing circumstances prevail.

Shop stewards also seem generally to prefer informal arrangements, but for quite different reasons. In the first place they provide them with an area of continued debate and negotiation. If conditions change they can then argue that former understandings are no longer relevant. Informal arrangements are also sometimes accepted by stewards because this is the only way in which the management can be persuaded to make a concession. Stewards, therefore, will accept the concession knowing that if they demanded a more formal arrangement the concession would be withdrawn. Finally there are certain issues which, according to the formal terms of the negotiating procedure agreement, might be regarded as managerial prerogatives, but about which the management, when faced with strong trade union pressure, is prepared to negotiate. Informal arrangements acceptable to both sides are then made. This compromise is thus based upon a mutual recognition of strength.

One particular problem which exists in many firms where there is a well-developed system of workshop bargaining is that the lower levels of supervision, notably the workshop foremen, tend to be by-passed in the process of negotiations. This is much more the responsibility of management than of the unions. Shop stewards cannot reasonably be blamed for seeking to resolve grievances as quickly as possible and for ventilating them with those who have the authority to take decisions. Management equally may find that it is preferable to channel the presentation of grievances and claims through the personnel department so that they receive immediate attention from persons who are skilled in dealing with problems of this kind. On the other hand, it is essential that the lower levels of supervision should be kept adequately informed of what is happening. It is for the management to work out how this can be achieved. Any failure to do this is likely to lead to considerable dissatisfaction.

The development of workshop bargaining has also presented the unions with new problems. In many unions the branches are based on the place of residence of the members and not on the establishments in which they are employed. Workshop problems tend, therefore, not to be discussed at branch level but instead become the sole concern of whatever workshop organization might exist, and, in particular, of the stewards. In most medium-sized and large firms there now exist joint shop stewards' committees where stewards not only of one union but of all the unions represented in the factory meet together for the discussion of current problems and sometimes for the determination of common action.

The extent to which provision is made for the integration of shop stewards in the formal structure of unions varies between one union and another. The separation between branch organization and workshop organization is, however, sometimes more apparent than real. Frequently the stewards at workshop level also play an important part in branch life and are often themselves branch officers. Nevertheless, the degree of control and authority exercised by unions over shop stewards, and particularly shop stewards' committees, is less – and perhaps inevitably less – than over trade union branches. In recent years a number of unions have tried to bring the stewards into closer touch with their own formal structure. Some unions provide for regular district meetings of stewards and others provide for training courses of various kinds. A number of unions also issue guide-books and other forms of literature to assist stewards in their everyday work as trade union lay representatives.

In the spring of 1963 the British Employers' Confederation and the Trades Union Congress issued a joint statement on the training of shop stewards. This statement recalled that representatives of the two organizations held a first discussion on the training of shop stewards in the early autumn of 1962. It was then generally agreed that in industries where there were shop stewards or their equivalent there was a need to increase the amount of training so that more stewards could obtain a broader understanding of their functions and responsibilities. The two organizations further agreed that it would help to increase the number of those willing to be trained if more training could be given during working hours. It was recognized that this training was primarily the task of the trade unions but that where questions of release with pay arose employers should be consulted about the syllabuses.

The 1963 joint statement of the B.E.C. and the T.U.C. went on to envisage an extension of shop steward training. The T.U.C. said that it would advise unions to consider discussing with employers and their organizations the possibility of arranging courses for stewards on the basis of release from work with pay. The B.E.C. undertook to inform its members of the action being taken by the T.U.C. and to recommend the possibility of extending the cooperation between employers, unions, and educational organizations or institutions with the object of providing more courses for shop stewards.

Joint Consultation

By joint consultation is meant the discussion between management and workers of matters which are of mutual concern and interest but which are not normally the subject of collective bargaining. There were few examples of joint consultation before the Second World War but it received a tremendous stimulus during the War when there was a strong national interest in increasing production for the defeat of Germany, Italy, and Japan. At that time much of the drive for the formation of joint production committees came from the more militant shop stewards. This pressure from below, from the militant section of the rank and file, began shortly after the German invasion of the U.S.S.R. in 1941. By the end of the War there was hardly an engineering factory of any size where a joint production committee was not in existence.

After the War the Government encouraged the existence of joint consultative arrangements in order to stimulate output. Provision for joint consultation was also contained in the main Acts of Parliament which nationalized a number of basic industries.

Despite this official encouragement joint consultative committees have declined both in number and in significance in the years since the ending of the Second World War. It is noticeable that joint consultation at factory level, through formal consultative committees as distinct from negotiating committees, has declined in parallel with the growth in the number of shop stewards, shop steward influence, and the extent of workshop bargaining.

One of the main reasons for the decline of joint consultation at factory level is that in normal peacetime conditions in private industry the workers have not the same dominant interest to increase production. In peacetime it is the differences of interest between employers and workers, rather than their mutual interest, which are more likely to be of prime concern to shop stewards. Many active shop stewards take the view that so long as the main motive of private industry is to maximize private profit they, as workers' representatives, have a fundamentally different interest to pursue.

Moreover, in joint consultation the ultimate decision always rests with the management. It is of the essence of consultation that there is no bargaining – as it is generally understood in industrial relations – and that there are no sanctions if either side cannot get its way. In his research paper for the Royal Commission, Dr McCarthy pointed out that the notion of joint consultation involves a paradox which stewards find difficult to accept. It presupposes that there are certain areas of management activity, for example wage-fixing, which are fit and proper subjects for joint determination by collective bargaining, but, on the other hand, there are other areas which although they may be discussed with workers' representatives must remain the exclusive prerogative of management. The paradox is even sharper when it is recalled that the subjects on which it is the practice to reach agreement through bargaining are the subjects on which there are supposed to be differences of interest between employers and workers. On the other hand, the subjects which are reserved for the exclusive decision of management are the subjects on which there is supposed to be a common interest and which are, therefore, suitable for joint consultation.

Although the importance of joint consultation at workplace level had generally declined in the postwar period there are, nevertheless, numerous joint committees at higher levels on which representatives of employers and trade unions sit together. The most recently appointed of all is the National Economic Development Council and the various committees which exist beneath it. There is also the National Joint Advisory Council to the Minister of Labour. This has been in existence since the beginning of the Second World War. There is also a wide range of other committees concerned with economic, industrial, and social matters on which trade unions and employers' organizations are represented. Thus, the machinery of joint consultation is generally more effective at national and regional level than it is at workplace level. Its diminishing importance at workplace level is due fundamentally to the fact that it has failed to evoke any strong interest or enthusiasm either from management or workpeople.

100 per cent Trade Union Organization

Unions seek to establish 100 per cent membership amongst all who are eligible to join because they believe that this strengthens them in collective bargaining. In the eyes of the trade union movement a minority of non-unionists in an establishment damages the interest not only of the non-unionists themselves but also of the majority who accept the obligations of trade union membership. A minority of non-unionists, say trade unionists, can be exploited by a management to the detriment of all the workpeople in an establishment. Moreover, the existence of a minority of non-unionists who, nevertheless, enjoy the benefits of agreements negotiated by the union, provides a standing temptation to the less scrupulous workers to drop out of the union. They see that they can obtain many of the benefits of trade union organization without contributing in any way to its maintenance.

It has been estimated that nearly 4 million workers in Britain are now employed in establishments where trade union membership is obligatory. The term 'closed shop' is, however, to some extent misleading. It suggests that only persons who are already members of a particular union can obtain employment in the particular workplace where the closed shop exists. In the great majority of cases this is not so. In most 100 per cent shops trade union membership is obligatory once a person has started work, but it does not prevent a non-unionist from obtaining employment providing that he indicates that he is prepared to join the union and is otherwise eligible for membership. The number of establishments where there is a closed shop in the strict sense, namely, that only persons who are already members of a particular union can secure employment, is only a minority of the total number of establishments where there is obligatory 100 per cent trade union membership. The industry in which there are more closed shops, in the strict sense, than any other is probably printing. The term 'union shop' is more appropriate than 'closed shop' for the majority of those establishments in Britain where there is obligatory trade union membership.

Another argument which is used by trade unionists in favour of 100 per cent membership is that it is socially immoral for a worker to take the benefits of trade union agreements without making any contribution towards the maintenance of trade union organization. Active trade unionists liken the attitude of non-unionists to that of a citizen who takes a ride on a municipal bus but refuses to pay his fare and expects other citizens to maintain the service.

Many employers, when first approached for the introduction of obligatory trade union membership, are inclined to resist it. They argue that it is up to a union to maintain its own strength of organization and that, in any case, they would not wish to interfere with the civil right of a worker to belong or not to belong to a trade union. Some employers have, however, moved away from this view. They recognize that 100 per cent organization may bring a measure of stability to an establishment. Where there is a minority of non-unionists there is likely to be resentment towards them, and it is difficult to justify the attitude of men who accept the benefits of trade union agreements but refuse to pay trade union contributions. This ill feeling may lead to acts of non-co-operation by trade unionists towards non-unionists and in some cases may lead to stoppages of work. Some employers also accept that it is better, on balance, that a union should be able to speak in a fully representative capacity on behalf of the workers who are employed in an establishment. Obligatory trade union membership may also strengthen trade union discipline. For these reasons many employers who at first resisted obligatory trade union membership have now come to accept it and even to support it.

The problem of the relationship between a worker's obligations to his workmates and his civil right to act as he individually chooses is an extremely difficult one. Clearly in any kind of civilized community citizens must accept some limitations of their personal freedom. Freedom does not imply that a man can act in whatever way he wishes, irrespective of the effect of his actions on other citizens. Thus, for example, civil liberty does not imply that a citizen should be able to drive on the wrong side of the road or that he should have the right to empty his dustbin in the street. Similarly in a workplace a man who insists on his right not to co-operate with others who are members of a trade union cannot logically complain if trade unionists say that they are not prepared to co-operate with him. The right not to co-operate belongs just as much to workers who are trade union members as to workers who are non-unionists.

The problem presented by 100 per cent trade union membership in relation to individual rights was considered by the International Labour Organization when it was debating the right to organize. The majority view of the I.L.O. was that the 'right to organize' could not be equated with the so-called 'right not to organize'. The I.L.O. held that the right to organize for workers should be protected by the State because of the economic inequality between employers on the one hand and workers on the other.

When, however, individual workers choose not to organize they affect not only their own interests but the interests of others. The right to organize in trade unions is essentially a social right. The so-called right not to organize undermines the social rights of other workers and ought not therefore to be protected by international instrument.

There are, nevertheless, strong arguments for granting the right of conscientious objection to trade union membership. There have been a number of examples in recent years where unions have accepted the continued employment of a non-unionist who, because of a deeply held religious conviction, objects to membership of any kind of association. In such cases they have asked that the conscientious objector should pay the equivalent of the trade union subscription to a mutually agreed charity. This provides a guarantee that the conscientious objector is not merely seeking to avoid the financial obligation to contribute to the funds of the union.

4: Some Current Problems

In this section a brief review is made of some current problems of industrial relations.

Incomes Policy

Ever since the Second World War Britain has been grappling with the problem of how to achieve price stability in an economy of near full employment. Successive governments have sought by a wide variety of measures to arrest the steady upward trend in prices. Appeals have been made at different times to various sections of the community to exercise restraint in their demands; and deflationary measures have been introduced at intervals to reduce the demand on the nation's resources. Usually these periods of deflation, accompanied by rising unemployment, have then been followed by periods of reflation when the economy has again become overheated.

Towards the end of 1964 the Labour Government made a new and determined effort to introduce an incomes policy by voluntary means. It felt it necessary to embark on such a course because of the seriousness of Britain's balance of payments deficit. In 1964 this deficit amounted to more than £750 million. In other words, Britain was spending abroad, for imports, overseas investment, and Government commitments, substantially more than she was earning. Clearly this could not continue.

The Government argued that the most sensible way in which to close this gap would be to expand exports. This, however, could not be done if British goods were priced out of world markets because of the constant pressure inside Britain for higher wages, salaries, and dividends. Restraint was, therefore, essential to ensure that incomes did not rise faster than productivity. If this objective were not achieved the only alternative, in the Government's view, would have been a very substantial increase in unemployment. Britain would have had to close the gap in its balance of payments by severe deflation and by drastic cuts in imports.

The argument for an incomes policy was also presented on other grounds. When money incomes rise faster than productivity some sections of the community tend to gain more than others and some sections, particularly pensioners and those employed in services where there are no high profits, tend to be left behind. Thus, an inflationary situation leads to gross social injustice.

A third argument for an incomes policy is presented in terms of economic planning. Some measure of economic planning is now regarded by all political parties as essential if an even rate of economic growth is to be maintained. If planning is necessary, then, it is argued, it is quite impractical to insist that incomes should be left completely outside the mechanism of planning. The logical corollary of economic planning, it is claimed, is a planned incomes policy.

In the light of these arguments the Government, in December 1964, secured the co-operation of the T.U.C. and the principal employers' organizations for a joint statement of intent on productivity, prices, and incomes. This joint statement said that it was the Government's economic objective to achieve and maintain a rapid increase in output and real incomes combined with full employment. It went on to say that the Government's social objective was to ensure that the benefits of faster growth were distributed in a way which satisfied the claims of social need and justice. Britain, it said, must improve its balance of payments, encourage exports, and sharpen its competitive ability. The Government promised to prepare and implement a general plan for economic development which would have as its objective a sharp increase in productivity. The T.U.C. and the employers' organizations, in turn, accepted that British industry must be dynamic, that its prices must be competitive, and that increases in wages, salaries, and other forms of income should be kept in line with the increase in productivity.

Throughout 1965 and in the early part of 1966, despite the joint declaration of intent, prices continued to rise. Money incomes of all forms increased faster than output. Eventually in July 1966 the Prime Minister called for a drastic standstill. He said that the country needed a breathing-space of twelve months in which productivity could catch up with the excessive increases in incomes which had already taken place. The Government's broad intention was, therefore, to secure in the second half of 1966 a standstill in which increases in prices or in incomes would, as far as possible, be avoided altogether. The first half of 1967 was to be regarded as a period of severe restraint.

The Government proposed also to give statutory backing to what had previously been a voluntary early warning system of higher prices and impending claims for higher wages and salaries. The voluntary early warning system had been established with the somewhat hesitant co-operation of both the employers' organizations and the T.U.C. It provided for the setting up, by Royal Warrant, of a National Board for Prices and Incomes which would keep under review the general movement of prices and of money incomes of all kinds and would examine particular cases in order to advise whether or not the behaviour of prices or of wages, salaries or other money incomes was in the national interest, as defined by the Government after consultation with management and unions.

In the late summer and early autumn of 1966 Parliament debated and eventually passed the Prices and Incomes Act. This established the National Board for Prices and Incomes on a statutory basis. Part II of the Act, which can be introduced by Order in Council approved by Parliament, gives the Government power by further Order to require notice of proposed claims for improvements in terms and conditions of employment, settlements or awards, and proposed increases in prices and charges.

If a specific Order has been issued requiring the notification of claims covering certain employees, both the person who presents the claim and the employer or employers' association who receive it are under an obligation to report it within seven days. The obligation to report the claim is placed on both parties, but it may be discharged by either party. Once the claim has been notified to the Minister, negotiations can then proceed and a settlement can be concluded.

The Minister can, by Order, require that when a settlement is reached the employer must notify the Minister within seven days. There is then a thirty-day standstill on the implementation of the settlement. The Minister, if he so wishes, can refer the settlement to the Prices and Incomes Board in which case there can then be a further delay. This power of delay was later extended under the Prices and Incomes (No. 2) Act, 1967 (*see* below).

The Prices and Incomes Act makes it an offence for an employer to implement a settlement during a standstill period. It is also an offence for a trade union or other person to take, or threaten to take, any action with a view to compelling, inducing or influencing an employer to implement an award or settlement during a standstill

93

period. This action refers particularly to taking part or persuading others to take part in a strike.

Part IV of the Prices and Incomes Act enabled the Government to give legal effect to its standstill on prices and incomes. It was, however, only a temporary provision and lasted only for one year.

It was part of the Government's policy on the prices and incomes standstill that there should be not only no new agreements for higher pay or shorter hours during the second half of 1966, but that, in addition, any agreements previously entered into for improvements to take place in the second half of 1966 should be deferred. The Government requested that in all such cases the date of implementation should be deferred by six months.

The Government said that it was not their intention to prohibit negotiations on claims during the standstill period, but they insisted that no new agreements should take effect before 1 January 1967 at the earliest and that they should not take effect during the first half of 1967 unless they could be justified as falling within revised criteria for improvements. These revised criteria were published in a White Paper, *Prices and Incomes Standstill: Period of Severe Restraint*, published in November 1966.

The new criteria stated that the norm for the annual rate of increase in money incomes per head must remain at zero, and that increases in incomes could be justified only in exceptional cases. Two exceptions were outlined. The first was agreements designed to increase productivity and efficiency. It was, however, emphasized that employees covered by such agreements should make a direct contribution towards increasing productivity and that some of the benefits should accrue to the community as a whole in the form of lower prices or improvements in quality. The second exception was in respect of the lowest paid workers. The Government said that it would be necessary to ensure that any pay increases justified on this ground would have to be genuinely confined to the lowest paid workers and not passed on to other workers.

In a report published in December 1966 the National Board for Prices and Incomes listed seven stringent requirements which any new productivity deal must meet if it were to be brought, during the period of severe restraint, within the criteria laid down by the Government. The seven requirements were as follows:

1. It must be shown that the workers were making a direct contri-

bution towards increasing productivity by accepting more exacting work or a major change in working practices.

2. Forecasts of increased productivity must be derived by the application of proper work standards.

3. An accurate calculation of the gains and the costs must show that the total cost per unit of output, taking into account the effect on capital, would be reduced.

4. The scheme should contain effective controls to ensure that the projected increase in productivity is achieved and that payment is made only as productivity increases or as changes in working practice take place.

5. There should be a clear benefit to the consumer in lower prices or in improved quality.

6. An agreement covering part of a plant must bear the cost of consequential increases elsewhere in the plant if any have to be granted.

7. In all cases negotiators must beware of setting extravagant levels of pay which would provoke resentment outside.

In March 1967 the Government published another White Paper outlining their policy on prices and incomes for the period after 30 June 1967. The Government said that they had two main objectives:

1. To create conditions favourable to sustained economic growth.

2. To work as quickly as possible towards the operation of an effective policy on a voluntary basis in agreement particularly with the C.B.I. and the T.U.C.

The Government said that they looked to all concerned to ensure that price increases should take place only after every effort had been made to absorb increases in costs. In relation to incomes, they said that the immediate need was to avoid a widespread and rapid increase in excess of the rise in national productivity. There could be no justification for returning to the norm of $3-3\frac{1}{2}$ per cent which prevailed up to July 1966. Any proposed increase in employment incomes would need to be justified against the following criteria:

1. Where the employees concerned, for example by accepting more exacting work or a major change in working practices, make a direct contribution towards increasing productivity in the particular firm or industry. Even in such cases some of the benefit should accrue to the community as a whole in the form of lower prices.

2. Where it is essential in the national interest to secure a change in the distribution of manpower (or to prevent a change which would otherwise take place) and a pay increase would be both necessary and effective for this purpose.

3. Where there is general recognition that existing wage and salary levels are too low to maintain a reasonable standard of living.

4. Where there is widespread recognition that the pay of a certain group of workers has fallen seriously out of line with the level of remuneration for similar work and needs in the national interest to be improved.

The White Paper stated that the Government's call for a standstill on company dividend distribution had been given full support by industry and commerce. The Government urged that, although the standstill was to end in July 1967, companies should continue to exercise moderation in distributions during the following year.

Finally, the White Paper emphasized that it was the firm intention of the Government to give every encouragement to the voluntary operation of their prices and incomes policy. They pointed out that Part IV of the Prices and Incomes Act, 1966, was due to lapse after one year. Nevertheless, the Government regarded it as necessary to maintain some limited reserve powers to enforce their policy. Accordingly they intended to activate Part II of the Prices and Incomes Act, 1966, and to strengthen their reserve powers over prices and incomes.

This strengthening of reserve powers, foreshadowed in the March 1967 White Paper, was contained in the Prices and Incomes (No. 2) Act, passed by Parliament later in 1967. The Act supplements the Government's powers to impose standstills on increases in prices or charges or the implementation of awards or settlements contained in Part II of the Prices and Incomes Act 1966. The Act provides for such standstills to be extended for a period not exceeding six months. This extension can be imposed by the Government only in cases on which there has been an adverse report by the National Board for Prices and Incomes. The new Act also provides legal immunity to employers who, during the periods of standstill and severe restraint, i.e. between 20 July 1966 and 1 July 1967, withheld pay increases which were due before or during this period.

The prices and incomes policy has not received universal support from either side of industry. There have been many who have been

doubtful of various aspects of the policy. The Government's deflationary measures have been widely criticized, and it has been argued
that the aim of achieving higher production has not been achieved.
Indeed, say the critics, the effect of the Government's policies has been
to slow down production, to cause a sharp reduction in the level of
capital investment, and to increase unemployment.

Some critics have also challenged the whole basis on which the
Government has made its analysis of Britain's economic problem.
These critics say that the balance-of-payments deficit was due mainly
to excessive Government overseas spending, principally for military
purposes. They urge that these commitments should be drastically
reduced. They also point out that, according to the available evidence,
wage and salary earnings in Britain have not been rising faster than
in other competing European industrial countries. On the contrary,
they have been rising more slowly than in other countries.

Some critics on both sides of industry have also expressed strong
doubts whether any system of statutory interference in price fixing
and income determination can be maintained other than for a very
short period. Prices and incomes, they say, are determined by
economic factors. No law can, in the long run, override the pressure
of these factors without causing serious distortions in the economy
leading eventually to disruption.

The Government claim that the measures which they have introduced, even though they recognize that they are drastic, are intended
to meet an emergency situation. The statutory controls, they say,
will be eased as the situation improves, but the need for a concerted
and generally accepted incomes policy will remain.

By the autumn of 1967 the main effects of the Government's
deflationary measures had become apparent. The total level of output
had been held down though there had been some increase in individual productivity. Production had been maintained even though
there had been a growth in unemployment. The number of workless
had risen to more than half a million, and it seemed likely that the
total would rise to three-quarters of a million or more by the middle
of the winter. Contrary to the hopes of the Government the main
decline in employment was in a number of manufacturing industries
and not in service occupations.

The balance-of-payments figures were open to different interpre-
tations. Some Government spokesmen claimed that Britain's balance-

of-payments had improved as a result of the Government's measures. The weight of economic opinion, however, seemed to be that the long-term problem had not been solved. Any stimulation of the economy sufficient to reduce substantially the number of unemployed would cause a fairly quick balance-of-payments crisis so long as Britain continued to maintain its existing overseas commitments.

The Government's decision to devalue the pound, taken at the end of 1967, followed by cuts in public expenditure announced in December 1967 and January 1968, were sure signs that the long-term balance-of-payments problem had not been solved. The Government indicated that in its next Budget consumer spending would be held down, and they called for continued restraint on incomes.

Trade Unionism and Law

The Royal Commission on Trade Unions and Employers' Associations was asked to give particular attention to the law affecting the activities of unions and employers' organizations. Numerous suggestions for changes in the law have been made.

From the employers' side, the Confederation of British Industry stated that for many years employers had felt that the greatest single contribution which could be made to the more effective working of the industrial relations system would be the better observance of agreements. It expressed sympathy for any proposed changes in the law which would have this effect. It commented that the most simple, and also the most radical, of such changes would be to make collective agreements enforceable at law. The C.B.I. recognized, however, that there were a number of strong objections to the introduction of legal enforceability of collective agreements. It limited itself, therefore, to an expression of hope that the Royal Commission would study further the possibility of legal enforcement of collective contracts in order to see whether there could be any combination of such enforcement with other desirable features of the British system which might be practical and which would substantially meet the doubts about legal enforceability raised by many employers.

The Engineering Employers' Federation submitted detailed proposals for a possible method of using legal sanctions to secure the observance of procedure agreements. It suggested that there should be a clear legal provision that workpeople who take strike or other action to coerce their employer before the applicable procedural arrangements have been fully utilized should be made liable by an independent tribunal to the imposition of fines.

Under the proposal of the Engineering Employers' Federation it was suggested that the decision to make charges about unconstitutional action before the tribunal should be taken by the appropriate employers' federation to which the employer belonged, and not by the employer himself. The Federation recognized that if an employer took proceedings, or if the decision lay with him as to whether proceedings should be taken against his own employees, industrial relations in his firm might be seriously damaged. If, however, the employer were not a member of his appropriate Federation he could be empowered to take the proceedings himself.

The tribunal, under the Engineering Employers' Federation's proposal, would be empowered to impose a fine on a worker for every day on which he took part in a strike or other action in breach of a procedure agreement. The tribunal would also be empowered to impose fines on unions if they did not take all reasonable steps to prevent or stop strikes in breach of agreement. The Federation accepted that fines should likewise be imposed on employers or employers' association who called a lockout in breach of a procedural obligation.

The Federation acknowledged that any system of fines which in practice could not be easily enforced would be of little value. It suggested, therefore, that any fines imposed by a tribunal should be deducted by the employer from the worker's wages. This deduction could be in instalments. If the worker changed his employer then a subsequent employer on notice from the tribunal would be bound to make the deduction from the worker's wages.

The British trade union movement is strongly opposed to the suggestion that collective agreements, including procedural agreements, should be enforceable at law. Their objection springs from their fundamental philosophy. The T.U.C., for example, has said that it cannot be over-emphasized that the effectiveness of obligations in industrial relations does not depend upon the existence of legal sanctions but on the common interest of both sides of industry in co-operating in an effective system of collective bargaining. The T.U.C. claims that its examination of systems of industrial relations in other countries shows that there is an inverse relationship between the practical significance of legal sanctions and the degree to which

H

industrial relations have reached a state of maturity. To make collective agreements of whatever kind enforceable at law would, in the view of the T.U.C., have a serious and damaging effect on industrial relations.

There are also a number of practical objections to the legal enforceability of agreements. These objections are by no means confined to the trade union movement. They have been voiced at various times by both sides of industry and by independent observers. Some of these objections are referred to in the evidence of the C.B.I. to the Royal Commission. The first is that if collective agreements were made enforceable at law unions would be tempted not to make any agreements at all. This is by no means as far fetched, particularly in relation to negotiating procedure agreements, as at first sight it might appear. There are a number of important industries in Britain where the negotiating arrangements for well-organized groups of workers are determined not by a written agreement but by long-established custom and practice. Unions which are well organized would be able to enforce negotiating rights without having to accept written obligations under a procedure agreement.

A second practical objection is that if, in the last resort, the Courts were charged with the task of enforcing agreements the effect might be to undermine the collective sense of responsibility of both sides of industry. An essential feature of the British system of industrial relations is that our arrangements are voluntary and are based on the principle that collective bargaining can be made to work because it is in the mutual interests of employers and workers that it should work.

The third practical objection is that to introduce the legal enforceability of agreements might bring the Courts into a whole range of industrial issues which, at present, are settled flexibly by the common sense and understanding of the parties directly involved. Experience in other countries, particularly in the U.S.A., shows that once the law is introduced into industrial relations there is virtually no limit to the range of issues which fall ultimately to be decided by the Courts. This would not be acceptable either to employers or to workers' organizations in this country.

The fourth practical objection is that the imposition of legal penalties on workers has never yet promoted good industrial relations. Workers who engage in strike action feel, rightly or wrongly, that they are protesting against an injustice. In this sense their action is completely different from that of a person who committs a criminal act. People who steal money know that they are doing wrong. A man who strikes with a view to securing the redress of a grievance feels that he is the victim and not the perpetrator of injustice. In any case, if thousands of workers are involved in a strike in breach of procedure it is difficult to imagine how a penalty could be enforced against all of them. Even if they were all fined they might then strike in protest against the penalty. What further penalty could then be imposed and enforced? The plain answer is that the law is not a suitable instrument to deal with an industrial situation of this kind.

The fifth practical objection is that if agreements were to be made legally enforceable it would be difficult to resist the argument that agreements between union members should also be legally enforceable. Unions would be able to enforce a strike decision by legal action and would be able to secure legal backing for fines against indiscipline. They would also be able to enforce the payment of arrears of subscriptions. None of these things would be welcomed either by employers or unions.

The trade union movement has asked for a number of changes in the law. A number of unions have expressed particular concern at the implications of recent Court decisions to the effect that the protection given to trade unionists in trade disputes does not extend to actions which induce a breach of commercial contract. This is of special importance because it has been held that labour-only contracts, for example in the construction industry, are not contracts of employment. Thus, union officials were not protected when, in the course of a trade dispute, they were held to have procured a breach of commercial contract. As the law now stands it appears that it is possible to obtain an injunction to restrain trade union strike action if it can be shown that the purpose of the strike action is to procure the breach of a commercial contract. Clearly this has serious implications for the trade union movement. In many industrial disputes it could be argued that the purpose of the union in taking strike action is to interfere with the commercial contracts of the employer against whom the dispute is being conducted.

The T.U.C. has also made it clear that it does not wish to see any extension of the period of legal standstill on pay awards and settlements made possible by the Prices and Incomes Acts. This, said the

T.U.C. in its evidence to the Royal Commission, would be an intolerable position if it lasted for any length of time.

One of the most recent suggestions made by the T.U.C. is that provision should be made for the representation of trade unionists on the boards of directors of firms. The T.U.C. argues that one of the most significant trends in recent years in the organization of industry has been the developing use of scientific techniques of management. The management function has become increasingly specialized. Many questions of close concern to workers cannot usefully be discussed in the absence of the executives whose responsibility it is to take decisions on questions affecting production. For this reason, says the T.U.C., trade unionsts must obtain representation at the various levels at which decisions are made. The T.U.C. has *not* suggested that legislation for trade union representation on the board of directors should make such representation mandatory. Legislation of a discretionary character, the T.U.C. says, would, however, be widely welcomed. It hopes that if legislation of this kind were introduced, the C.B.I., as the representative body of employers, would take a strong lead in encouraging its members to follow the spirit of the proposal. The real object, according to the T.U.C., would be to encourage companies to recognize and take advantage of the mutual benefits to be obtained from more active participation by trade union representatives in company policy and day-to-day practice.

Some unions have urged that legal effect should be given to the I.L.O. Conventions on the right to organize and the right to bargain collectively. These unions recognize that it would still be desirable, as far as possible, to keep issues out of the normal Courts. They suggest that this would be achieved by utilizing the Industrial Court for the enforcement of these rights. New legislation, it is suggested, could provide that complaints that the right to organize was not being observed should be submitted in the first place to the employer against whom the complaint was made. If the complaint was not resolved by this direct approach or through whatever joint machinery might exist in the section of industry concerned it could then be submitted to the Ministry of Labour so as to secure the assistance of the conciliation service. If this still proved abortive the complaint could then be submitted to the Industrial Court. It would be for the Industrial Court to deal with the complaint by whatever method it thought most appropriate. It could enquire and report on the complaint. Alternatively, it could conciliate or mediate between the parties so as to promote a voluntary settlement. Finally, it could, if necessary, issue an award that the right to organize should be observed. This right would then become an implied term of the contract and, if necessary, could be enforced in a normal Court of Law. The whole point of this procedure would, however, be as far as possible to keep issues of this kind away from the normal Courts and to keep them within the machinery of the Industrial Court. The power to make complaints would rest with representative organizations of workers and employers.

Among other suggestions made by trade unions for changes in the law was one that certain provisions of the Merchant Shipping Acts should be repealed. Some of these provisions were said to be outdated and to prejudice the rights of seamen. At the time of the seamen's strike in 1966 the Government acknowledged that the Merchant Shipping Act should be revised.

Unions have also been concerned to defend the right to picket. They have expressed concern at Court decisions which might be interpreted as suggesting that some limitation could be imposed on the number of workers who might lawfully engage in peaceful picketing.

The T.U.C. has also asked for the reintroduction of arbitration at the request of one party to a dispute after the normal negotiating machinery has been exhausted. This would require new legislation on the lines of the former Industrial Disputes Order.

Labour Courts

An interesting development in recent years has been the creation of what is, in effect, a system of labour courts outside the normal Courts of Law. These courts, known as Industrial Tribunals, have functions of adjudication under the Contracts of Employment Act, 1963, the Industrial Training Act, 1964, the Redundancy Payments Act, 1965, and the Selective Employment Payments Act, 1966.

The Tribunals were established under the Industrial Training Act, 1964. Their function under that Act is to adjudicate on minor disputes concerning training levies imposed on employers. The Tribunals consist of three members. One is a lawyer, one is drawn from a panel of employers' organizations, and the other from employees' organizations. The Tribunals are also empowered under the Redundancy Payments Act to adjudicate on disputes about payments to employees and rebates to employers from the Redundancy Fund. Under the Contracts of Employment Act an employee who is dissatisfied because no written particulars have been given to him, or because the written particulars are inadequate, may require the matter to be referred to the Industrial Tribunal. The Tribunal has the power to determine what particulars should be included in the statement so as to comply with the requirements of the Act. Under the Selective Employment Payments Act, 1966, employers whose establishments have been refused registration for payment of premium or refund may appeal to the Industrial Tribunal. They may also appeal against a decision by the Minister to remove an establishment from the register, or against the amount of payment which the Minister proposes to make.

Professor K. W. Wedderburn has also pointed out that various other oddments of jurisdiction have now been allocated to the Industrial Tribunals. According to an article which he wrote in *New Society* on 9 December 1965, disputes, mainly concerning employees of nationalized industry, previously heard by various referees and boards under no less than twenty-three different statutes have all now been transferred to the Industrial Tribunals. The Minister of Labour's evidence to the Royal Commission justifiably commented that the nucleus of a system of labour courts exists essentially in these Industrial Tribunals.

Restrictive Practices

There is probably no definition, acceptable both to employers' organizations and to trade unions, of what constitutes a 'restrictive practice'. The C.B.I. has defined 'a restrictive labour practice' as any work practice, collectively operated, which hinders or acts as a disincentive to the more effective use of labour, technical skill, machinery or other resources. The problem created by restrictive practices is, in the view of the C.B.I., essentially one of over-manning or of the under-utilization of manpower resources.

In the view of many employers restrictive practices not only have an immediate effect in causing inefficiency, but they are also conducive to restrictive or obstructionist attitudes among workers. This has led, says the C.B.I., to general resistance to technical innovation;

insistence by unions on the maintenance of rigid manning scales; demarcation rules, often unrealistic in relation to modern production techniques; and reluctance or refusal to accept changes in working arrangements, such as the introduction of shift work required to make a new plant or process economically worth while.

Employers have never claimed that restrictive practices apply equally throughout British industry. Within the engineering group of industries, for example, the Engineering Employers' Federation has said that 'the position varies enormously not only as between districts but also as between establishments. In some firms blatant restrictive practices are unknown where in others, they are all too common'. In London newspaper production it is now generally acknowledged that there is widespread over-manning.

The attitude of the British trade union movement towards restrictive practices is generally very different from that of employers. Many unions, for example, dislike the term 'restrictive practice' and prefer instead to speak of 'trade practice' or the autonomous regulation of the requirements of the job. They argue that in almost every kind of occupation it is necessary to establish and then to observe certain practices to ensure that jobs are performed by people who are properly qualified and who have the necessary skill. This, it is said, is necessary, moreover, to maintain standards of quality. The unions also claim that certain practices have to be established for the protection of the safety, health, and welfare of workers and to prevent exploitation.

The unions point out that it is not only workpeople in industry who establish and maintain practices for the regulation of their jobs. All the professions insist on much stricter regulations for the control of their respective occupations. The professions, even more than the unions, are concerned to prevent the dilution of skill, and they observe practices which sometimes appear to the public to have little to commend them but which nevertheless on careful examination can be shown to be relevant to the maintenance of proper professional standards.

Some restrictive practices arise from an underlying fear of unemployment. This is particularly the case in industries where there is a tradition of heavy unemployment, such, for example, as in ship-building. Insistence on trade demarcation is much more an expression of a determination on the part of workers to keep their jobs than to retard production. The unions claim that the case against demarcation is frequently over-stated. Demarcation, they point out, may be only another way of providing for the division of labour. It was the employers and not the unions who first insisted on the division of labour as a necessary contribution to greater efficiency.

The unions also argue that the restrictive practices of some trade associations and near-monopolies are far more damaging to the economy and to economic growth than the practices of trade unions. Monopolistic practices may result in the less than optimum use of resources, a failure to develop new methods, the maintenance of unnecessarily high prices, and stringent restrictions on competitive trading.

The Engineering Employers' Federation has made proposals for the examination of restrictive labour practices by an independent tribunal. It has proposed that the tribunal which investigates such practices should have power to issue an order requiring those insisting on or supporting a restrictive practice to desist therefrom. Any breach of such order could be followed by the imposition of penalties.

There is probably no simple formula for dealing with restrictive trade practices. The unions would certainly claim that many of them can be justified on broad social grounds. The C.B.I. in its evidence to the Royal Commission acknowledged that 'not all so-called restrictive labour practices can be condemned out of hand'. Other restrictive practices are the outcome of unemployment or bad industrial relations and can only be overcome over a period of time by the creation of new conditions which give confidence to workpeople. This, like so many other problems in the field of industrial relations, is one that can hardly be resolved by law. There are still other restrictive practices which it would be difficult to justify on any grounds. They are sometimes intended to preserve the position of a particular group of skilled workers whose role in industry is being undermined by new technical developments.

The report of the Royal Commission will, when published, no doubt have something to say about restrictive practices. It may conclude that some of them, on balance, are not harmful but are intended to serve a worthy purpose. Of those which cannot be justified the Commission will have to consider how best to deal with them: by patient negotiation, the creation of confidence among workers and full employment; or by a tribunal on the lines advocated by the Engineering Employers' Federation. One thing, however, is certain. If there is unemployment, neither patient negotiations, industrial sanctions, nor even the force of the law will overcome the restrictive attitude of workers who are struggling to keep their jobs.

A Short Bibliography

The following books cover the main aspects of industrial relations and deal with contemporary problems.

A. Flanders, *Trade Unions* (Hutchinson, 1960)

A. Flanders and H. Clegg, *The System of Industrial Relations in Great Britain* (Blackwell, 1964)

C. Jenkins and J. E. Mortimer, *British Trade Unions Today* (Pergamon, 1965)

C. Jenkins and J. E. Mortimer, *The Kind of Laws the Unions Ought to Want* (Pergamon, 1968)

I.L.O., *The Trade Union Situation in the United Kindom* (I.L.O., 1961)

B. C. Roberts (*editor*), *Industrial Relations – Contemporary Problems and Perspectives* (Methuen, 1962)

Evidence to the Royal Commission on Trade Unions and Employers' Associations: Trades Union Congress; Ministry of Labour; Engineering Employers' Federation; Confederation of British Industry (H.M.S.O., 1966–7)

Royal Commission on Trade Unions and Employers' Associations, Research Papers (H.M.S.O., 1966–7):

1. *The Role of Shop Stewards in British Industrial Relations* – W. E. J. McCarthy
2. *Disputes Procedures in British Industry* – A. I. Marsh
3. *Industrial Sociology and Industrial Relations* – A. Fox
4. *Productivity Bargaining and Restrictive Labour Practices* – Anon
5. *Trade Union Structure and Government* – J. Hughes
6. *Trade Union Growth and Recognition* – G. S. Bain
7. *Employers' Associations* – V. G. Munns and W. E. J. McCarthy

K. W. Wedderburn, *The Worker and the Law* (MacGibbon andKee, 1965)

E. Wigham, *What is Wrong with the Unions?* (Penguin, 1961)

H.M.S.O., *Industrial Relations Handbook* (new editions are published from time to time).

The following are more specialist works or deal with the history of trade unionism.

BIBLIOGRAPHY

V. L. Allen, *Militant Trade Unionism* (Merlin Press, 1966)

V. L. Allen, *Trade Unions and the Government* (Longmans, 1960)

V. L. Allen, *Power in Trade Unions* (Longmans, 1958)

W. A. Citrine, *Trade Union Law* (Stevens, 1960)

A. H. Clegg, A. Fox, and A. F. Thompson, *A History of British Trade Unions 1889 – 1910* (Oxford University Press, 1964)

H. Clegg, A. J. Killick, and R. Adams, *Trade Union Officers* (Blackwell, 1961)

K. Coates and A. Topham, *Industrial Democracy in Great Britain* (MacGibbon and Kee, 1968)

G. D. H. Cole, *Short History of the Working Class Movement* (Allen and Unwin, 1947)

J. Corina, *Incomes Policy: Problems and Prospects* (Institute of Personnel Management, 1966)

A. Flanders, *Industrial Relations – What is Wrong With the System* (Faber, 1965)

C. Grunfeld, *Modern Trade Union Law* (Sweet and Maxwell, 1966)

A. Hutt, *British Trade Unionism: A Short History – 1800–1961* (Lawrence and Wishart, 1962)

W. E. J. McCarthy, *The Closed Shop in Britain* (Blackwell, 1964)

A. Marsh, *Industrial Relations in Engineering* (Pergamon, 1965)

H. Pelling, *A History of British Trade Unionism* (Macmillan, 1963)

B. Roberts, *The Trades Union Congress 1868–1921* (Allen and Unwin, 1958)

B. Roberts, *Trade Union Government and Administration in Great Britain* (Allen and Unwin, 1956)

H. A. Turner, *Trade Union Growth Structure and Policy* (Allen and Unwin, 1962)

H. A. Turner, G. Clack, and G. Roberts, *Labour Relations in the Motor Industry* (Allen and Unwin, 1967)

S. and B. Webb, *Industrial Democracy* (Longmans, 1920)

Index

111